The SIDE *of* KINDNESS

Recovering the Lost Art of Being Kind

Sister Sandra Makowski

Copyright © by 2024 Sister Sandra Makowski

All rights reserved. This book or any of its portion may not be reproduced or transmitted in any means, electronic or mechanical, including recording, photocopying, or by any information storage and retrieval system, without the prior written permission of the copyright holder except in the case of brief quotations embodied in critical reviews and other noncommercial uses permitted by copyright law.

Printed in the United States of America
Library of Congress Control Number: 2024919879
ISBN: Softcover   979-8-89518-300-7
          e-Book   979-8-89518-301-4

Published by: WP Lighthouse
Publication Date: 09/18/2024

To buy a copy of this book, please contact:
WP Lighthouse
Phone: +1-888-668-2459
support@wplighthouse.com
wplighthouse.com

Dedication and Acknowledgements

This book is dedicated to my two sets of families: my family of origin, my mom, dad, and sister, and my family of the Sisters of St. Mary of Namur.

I dedicate this book to my mom, who taught me poetry at a very early age, plus patience, understanding, and laughter, how to endure the struggles of life with courage and optimism, and so much more. She was an author herself, a poet and lover of words. I am sure she is now proclaiming the Word out loud for all of the angels in heaven to hear.

I dedicate this book to my dad—he has had a challenging life and suffered much as a young boy at St. Mary's Home, and his many years as a postal worker were not easy either. His sense of humor won him many a battle, along with his love of music, ardent and enthusiastic conversation, and the Chicago Cubs. I have come to cherish him as my dad who will be forever my model of hard work, perseverance, constancy, and love.

I dedicate this book to my sister, Carole Jean, who is forever my twin whom I love with all my heart and can't wait to see again.

I also want to acknowledge Sister Colie Stokes in a special way, along with Sister Judy Carroll. Colie patiently withstood the many drafts of these chapters, offered her own wisdom and insight, and has been a true friend for 48 years. I thank her, along with Sister Judy Carroll—the three of us lived a lot of the stories that are recounted in this book, the memories of which will be forever part of who we are today.

Special acknowledgement goes to the following people. If it were not for the following people, this would not have been published. They supported me financially, along with prayers, support, encouragement, etc.

Introduction: *The Lost Art of Being Kind*. I dedicate this introduction, which I call "*The Lost Art of Being Kind*" to the Sisters of St. Mary of Namur—for everything they have taught me and have been for me, from my first day of school at the age of seven, until the present. They truly taught me the real meaning of the motto of the Sisters of St. Mary: "In the simplicity of my heart I have joyfully offered all to God."

**ced*Chapter Four: Let Your Yes Mean Yes*
Sister Canice Adams, SSCM and St. Gregory the Great School in Bluffton, South Carolina
Mr. Patrick Manna

Chapter Five: Break the Pattern of Bad Behavior
Sister Canice Adams, SSCM and St. Gregory the Great School in Bluffton, South Carolina

Chapter Eight: Discovering the Beautiful Is Discovering God
Sister Mary Joseph, OLM and the Sisters of Charity of Our Lady of Mercy
Bill and Joan Aselage
Sister Margaret Donner, SSMN

Chapter Nine: Rwanda—A Country of a Thousand Hills and a Thousand Faces of Kindness
Sister Marie Julianne Farrington, SSMN
Sister Marie Camille Uwamariya, SSMN
Sister Mary Veronica White, SSMN

Chapter Ten: What Do You Want to Be? How About a Saint?
Peter Shahid, who dedicates this to his parents, Albert P. and Julia K. Shahid
Sue Sudlik and Sister Beth Hays, SSMN
Cecilia Velte
Michael Curry

Chapter Eleven: Give Yourself the Gift of Patience
Sister Mary Hartley, SSMN

Chapter Twelve: The Art of Listening—We Have Two Ears and One Mouth for a Reason
Kathleen Heffern
Larisa Agrest

Chapter Thirteen: Knowing How to Fail May Lead You to Success
Charlie Ledford

Chapter Fourteen: Believe in the Impossible
Maria Aselage dedicates this to her parents, Bill and Joan Aselage, for "believing in me and loving me."
The Sisters of SS. Cyril and Methodius
Mr. Patrick Manna
Ron and Mary Schleich
John and Mary Sroda
Peter Shahid, who dedicates this to his parents, Albert P and Julia K. Shahid

Chapter Fifteen: You Don't Need a Pedometer to Make Every Step Count
Noreen Wall

Chapter Sixteen: Kindness—and a Canon Law Degree
Michael Foster
Joseph Klos
Buffalo Diocesan Tribunal
Catholic University of America's canon law graduating class of 1989

Chapter Seventeen: Prayer—a Rather Intense, and "In Tents," Experience
Father Jeffrey Kirby and the residents at Drexel House
The Sisters of Charity Foundation of South Carolina

Chapter Eighteen: Memory-Keepers
Deacon James Moore and Tina Moore

Chapter Nineteen: Where Have All the Manners Gone?
Andrea and David Marcella
Hannah Timmons
Monsignor Frank Hanley

Chapter Twenty-one: Finding Kindness Behind the Rolling Stone
Bishop Robert Cunningham, Bishop of Syracuse

Chapter Twenty-two: First-Class Women Are Not Second-Class Citizens
Holly Kasper and Kelly Timmons
Phyllis Atkins and the South Carolina Council of Catholic Women
Katrina Spigner
Bonny Butler

Chapter Twenty-three: Are You Just "One of the Girls" in the Office?
Katrina Spigner

Chapter Twenty-four: "Not Counting Women and Children" — Where's the Kindness in That?
Bishop Thompson dedicates this chapter to Sister Sandra Makowski "for her years of holy service to God and His Church." (Thank you, Bishop Thompson.)

Chapter Twenty-six: I May Not Be Perfect, but I Am Saved
Deacon Larry Roberts
Joan and Bill Aselage
Carol and Paul Timmons, Sr.
Paul Timmons and George Kasper

Chapter Twenty-seven: Hope Is Only a Rooftop Away
Dedicated to the founder and staff at the website www.churchannulment.com serving "Church annulment – another chance"

Chapter Twenty-eight: Because Others Are Mean Is No Reason Why I Should Be
Dr. Mitch Carnell

Chapter Twenty-nine: Don't Just Do Something, Stand There
Bill and Joan Aselage
Paul and Carol Timmons, Sr.
John M. Bleecker, Jr.
Father Jeffrey Kirby

Chapter Thirty: Hurray for Vatican Council II
Monsignor Frank Hanley

Chapter Thirty-two: Don't Worry—Be Happy
The Community of Felician Sisters in Kingstree, South Carolina dedicates this chapter to Sister Maryjane Golden, SSMN.

Chapter Thirty-four: Jesus Wants You to Enjoy the Danish
Marianna Williamson

Chapter Thirty-five: God Is the Side of Kindness
Bishop Robert E. Guglielmone, Bishop of Charleston

Contents

Introduction xv
I Don't Agree With You … So Shoot Me… 1
The Power of Good Morning 5
"Don't Bother Me Now" May Not Be the Best Response 8
Try Giving Up "Giving Up" This Lent (Lenten Reflection) 21
O Happy Fault! (Lenten Reflection) 25
Discovering the Beautiful Is Discovering God 28
Rwanda—A Country of a Thousand Hills and a Thousand Faces of Kindness 33
What Do You Want to Be? How About a Saint? 40
Give Yourself the Gift of Patience (Holiday Kindness) 45
The Art of Listening— We Have Two Ears and One Mouth for a Reason 49
Knowing How to Fail May Lead You to Success 53
Believe in the Impossible 57

You Don't Need a Pedometer to Make Every Step Count 61

Kindness— and a Canon Law Degree 65

Prayer: A Rather Intense, and "In Tents," Experience 69

Memory-Keepers 74

Where Have All the Manners Gone? 78

Better to Give a Blessing Rather Than the Finger 83

Finding Kindness Behind the Rolling Stone (Easter) 86

First-Class Women Are Not Second-Class Citizens 91

Are You Just "One of the Girls" in the Office? 97

"Not Counting Women and Children"—Where's the
Kindness in That? 100

Let's Move Our "But" 105

I May Not Be Perfect, But I Am Saved 108

Hope Is Only a Rooftop Away 112

Because Others Are Mean Is No Reason Why I Should Be ... 117

Don't Just Do Something, Stand There 122

Hurray for Vatican Council II 126

It's All in the Tone 131

Don't Worry—Be Happy 134

Dress for Success 139

Jesus Wants You to Enjoy the Danish 143

God Is the Side of Kindness 147

Endnotes 152

Introduction

ONCE UPON A TIME in a little village in India, there lived a kind old man who would pray every morning at the Ganges River. One morning as he was praying, his eyes landed on a poisonous spider that was struggling in the water. He cupped his hands to carry it ashore. As he placed the spider on the ground, it stung him. His prayers saved him from the results of the sting. However, the second day he returned to the river and the same thing happened. Finally, on the third day, this kind man was knee deep in the river, and sure enough, there was that same spider, legs frantic in the water. As the man went to lift the spider yet again, the spider said to him, "Why do you keep lifting me? Can't you see that I will sting you every time, because that is what I do?" And the kind man cupped his hands about the spider yet again, and replied, "Because that is what I do."[i]

In the book *The Book of Awakening*, where we find this story, Mark Nepo continues by stating that there are many reasons to be kind, but none is as compelling as the spiritual fact that it is what we do. It is how the inner organ of being keeps pumping. Spiders sting, wolves howl, ants build small hills that no one sees, and human beings lift each other up no matter the consequences. This is what it means to be human. To be human is to be kind despite the consequences. At other times, it may be the reaching out that is even more important than the sting.[ii]

If one were to search the internet, one would discover that there are over ten thousand books with the word "kindness" in their titles. There are banners made, symbols painted, songs sung, and poems recited all praising the role of kindness in our world, our neighbor, our planet.

According to this story, acts of kindness are what people do. It is what it means to be human—it is what people write about, sing about, and proclaim. Why then would I write a book about kindness? What can I possibly say about being kind that has not already been said, digested, proclaimed in song, and painted in symbol? It's certainly not because I haven't experienced kindness in my life. I have lived a life surrounded by kindness. My family taught me at a young age to be kind to the new neighbors across the street because they are strangers and that's what we do. They taught me to help Mrs. Standish because she is elderly and needs someone to sweep her stairs. Why? Because that is what we do. They taught me that if everyone makes fun of Geraldine because she is different from the rest of the class—so, invite her over to the house for dinner. Why? Because that is what we do. It's as simple as that. We are kind because that is what we do. I grew up with kindness and I entered a religious community that continued to show me what it means to be kind. Perhaps because I was surrounded by this care, I became more sensitive to moments when the care was not there.

So, what more is there to say that has not already been said about the topic? Actually, there may be absolutely nothing new to say that has not already been said. But I have been drawn to this topic because I am actually surprised when I find myself in the presence of

Introduction

kindness. It didn't used to be that way for me, but lately I feel like the world is changing. Now, when I am in the presence of kindness, it appears to be more like an act of heroism rather than a simple human response. This is the question that I have been left pondering for quite some time. What has happened to kindness in our world? Why does kindness sometimes appear to me to be on the endangered species list? Is kindness becoming a lost art? Has it gone out of style, and, if so, why?

There appears to be a lot of meanness in our world. I don't get it. I don't understand harsh words, mean-spirited actions, and nastiness. I don't understand swearing, foul language, bullying, or intolerance toward others who attempt to express a different opinion or point of view. Don't get me wrong. I am sure that I have had my share of righteousness at times, and I have my moments when I want to shove someone under a bus. But it is usually because I have come face to face with cruelty, and I have become pierced by its pain and its sting and its evil force. Common courtesy seems to be pretty uncommon, whereas violence and meanness have become contagious.

I began writing a series of columns at my workplace regarding etiquette and manners. When looking back at what I had written, I then realized that all the columns had one underlying theme, woven as a quilt throughout the writings. That theme was the theme of kindness. The subject matter varied. There were topics regarding courtesy, civility, gratitude, listening, manners, etc. But they all related to how we treat each other. In the end, this book is the result. If we choose the path of kindness, we choose the path that leads to God. I believe that God is not only *on* the side of kindness, God *is* the side of kindness.

So, I invite you to take this journey with me—the journey of recovering kindness in our world. If we can recover kindness, then we can take its side. Let us put away our prejudice, our need to win every battle of words, and our need to put someone down or disregard the feelings and needs of those around us. Let us put aside every harsh and mean-spirited word that spills from our mouths, and let us walk together on this journey where God's Word will flow from our mouths instead of words that kill and smother another human being's reputation. Let us allow God's words to be our words, our melody of action in the daily walk of life. Then our journey to recover kindness will become automatic, like the wise man who reached to save the spider no matter the consequence. It is what we do. Let's together form a kindness crusade. We will never lose the battle if we choose the winning side—the side of kindness.

SAVING KINDNESS

Faceless and frantic, Running and weaving
In and out of people's lives…as well as ones' own.
Dropped paper, garbage on the streets, as well as an empty shell that once held a life.

Searching for softness, and generosity, a smile, or even just a nod of notice
A gift of gratitude
  A thank-you
    A door being opened
      A child held in love
        A sadness transformed into a revelation
          A window of giving – a truth exposed
            A life turning toward wholeness once again.
One window, One touch, One step, One glance
Won over,
By one small gesture. That's not asking for too much is it?
One small glimmer of hope
That the world has not given up on kindness.
    —Sandra Makowski

1

I Don't Agree With You … So Shoot Me…

"Be beautiful if you can, wise if you want to. But be respected—that is essential."
—Anna Gould

"I must respect the opinions of others even if I disagree with them."
—Herbert Henry Lehman

"If you have some respect for people as they are, you can be more effective in helping them to become better than they are."
—John W. Gardner

"Be devoted to one another in brotherly love; give preference to one another in honor."
—Romans 12:10 NASB

"To sum up, all of you, be harmonious, sympathetic, brotherly, kindhearted, and humble in spirit."
—1 Peter 3:8 NASB

The Side of Kindness

EVERY WEDNESDAY MORNING for three years, I would drive to the nursing home not far from where I lived and spend the morning with my mother. My mother lived three years in this nursing facility before she died, and we spent many treasured moments together. We did have one weekly ritual that we followed without fail, and that was our trip to the IHOP for pancakes. We would order our usual—mine was pancakes, eggs over easy, bacon crispy, and whole-wheat toast, and hers was one blueberry pancake with strawberry jam. (Who had the biggest appetite???) We would both order coffee, and then she would be ready to make a toast. We would raise our coffee cups and recite these words while clicking our coffee cups together:

>Here's to you and here's to me
>May we never disagree.
>But if we do
>The h---- with you
>Here's to me.

We would laugh ourselves silly, because, of course, that was the closest my mother ever came to swearing in her life. She would always look around to make sure no one had heard her, and she would revel in her little rebellion against niceness. Oh, I loved her so.

Lately, however, I've been thinking about the words of our weekly rebellion against niceness, and how they seem truer now than ever before. How do we really feel about people who disagree with us, or have a differing opinion? What kind of society have we become when we no longer allow or even care to hear viewpoints or opinions different from our own? Why is that? Why do we want to simply surround ourselves with people who think like we do and, in doing so, shut ourselves off from broadening our perspectives, opinions, and points of view? Why do people (including myself) often assume that everyone should agree with their way of thinking and, if they don't, then there is something wrong with them?

There was once a popular song, written by Malvina Reynolds but made famous by Pete Seeger in 1963, called "Little Boxes." Here are some of the lyrics:

> "Little boxes on the hillside,
> Little boxes made of ticky tacky
> Little boxes on the hillside,
> Little boxes all the same,
> There's a pink one and a green one
> And a blue one and a yellow one
> And they're all made out of ticky tacky
> And they all look just the same."[iii]

The song continues with a few more verses, but you get the idea. It was very popular during the 1960s era, when there was a strong movement in society against conformism. Malvina Reynolds, who died in 1978, was a social activist and writer of protest songs. She wrote this song as a political statement about the uniformity, the sameness, that she believed was fostered by what are now known as "cookie-cutter" or "tract" houses; houses along suburban streets with identical floor plans. I heard this song last week and it was the first time in years that I heard it or even thought about it.

However, I found myself asking the question, are we willing to listen to and respect those who think differently, or have we succumbed to living out the words to this song: "and we all look (act, think, believe) just the same"?

Have you noticed that many talk show hosts have callers who introduce themselves as "ditto heads"? Is that because they are only listening to the show because they already know that they will agree with the opinion of the talk show host?

It seems to me that disagreement between and among people is meaner than ever before. This is very noticeable when reading people's blogs, Facebook pages, etc. The language used and the forcefulness behind the words seem filled with anger, even rage, especially toward someone who has a different viewpoint from one's own, or some issue that is contrary to one's own way of thinking.

Why can't disagreements be viewed as healthy and acceptable as long as they are reasonable and realistic? People think differently, and it is important to respect as well as encourage different opinions and points of view. Allowing people to disagree should not be looked upon as offensive or stupid. If we can't enter into respectful debate on issues of importance, then how can we expect to grow, change, understand each other better, be more compassionate, and give rise to a kinder, gentler world,? So—in this kinder world that we view with longing, can we resolve to listen more carefully, be willing to listen and be open to another point of view, and be willing to compromise if necessary? And maybe someone, after respectfully listening to a different point of view, will say to us, "Thanks, I never thought of it that way before."

CONSIDER THE FOLLOWING

- Can you remember a time you offered a different point of view, either in a group setting or a discussion? Can you remember the reaction from the group? Was it respectful or upsetting? Did it lead to fruitful discussion or closed opposition?

- Are there times when you felt like you were just a "little box" among other "little boxes"? Please explain.

- How can kindness be practiced when either listening to another point of view or introducing another point of view into the discussion?

2

The Power of Good Morning

"Grace to you and peace from God our Father and the Lord Jesus Christ."
—1 Corinthians 1:3 NIV

"Greet one another with a holy kiss."
—Romans 16:16 NIV

"If you have only one smile in you, give it to the people you love. Don't be surly at home, then go out in the street and start grinning 'Good morning' at total strangers."
—Maya Angelou

"You've got to get up every morning with a smile on your face, and show the world all the love in your heart, then people gonna treat you better. You're gonna find, yes, you will, that you're beautiful as you feel."
—Carole King

WHAT HAS HAPPENED to "good morning"? Has that disappeared along with acts of kindness? I remember recently being in an office where the same two workers came into work every day, sat three feet from each other, and never acknowledged the other.

Is it that difficult to say "hello" or "good morning" to people you meet, or people you work with? I began to wonder if the same people where I worked felt that they would be charged a fee for saying good morning. After all, they had been sharing the same office oxygen for years.

Saying good morning should not be difficult. It consists of two simple words. No one is asking anyone to bow, salute, kneel, or curtsey. Even a casual nod or mumble would be a lot better than the nothing that occurs at far too many work sites anymore. I have noticed that the pet dog receives a much better greeting than humans. I realize that many people get along a lot better with pets than with people, but really, acknowledging that the other person exists is Communication 101.

So... let's consider beginning our day with the words "good morning"!! Let's try saying it to people we live with and work with, and let's mean it when we say it. It helps to maintain the standard of civility that we are all entitled to in the workplace and home. First of all, it's free and it doesn't cost a thing. Second of all, when we greet people with a good morning, we are actually giving them a blessing. We are telling them that we hope they will have a good morning. This is why, if you ever meet a grumpy person who responds to your "good morning" with a line such as "Who said it was good?" their response, besides being rude, is actually inaccurate. We are not defining the morning by saying "good morning"; rather, we are offering a blessing that this person may be blessed with a very good day. And that, my dear reader, is a very kind thing to do.

When we see a fellow human being, we are obliged to acknowledge their value and importance. Once you have said it, this can set a tone for the rest of the day. You have blessed the person you are working with. May you be blessed with a good dose of hospitality to begin your day!

So—Good Morning, and, as Mary Oliver states in her poem "Why I wake early": "Watch, now, how I start the day / In happiness, in kindness."[iv]

> GOOD MORNING
> Namaskaram
> Bunã ziua
> Bon jour
> Bon giorno
> Guten Morgen
> Buenos dias
> Bon dia
> Dobroe utro

CONSIDER THE FOLLOWING

- Does it make a difference in your day if someone greets you? Does it depend on how they greet you—with sincerity, or a dose of obligation?

- How about if someone ignores you—does that also make a difference in your day?

- In our search for kindness, can we find it in the way we greet each other? What are the different ways we can greet each other?

3

"Don't Bother Me Now" May Not Be the Best Response

"Circumstances may cause interruptions and delays, but never lose sight of your goal. Prepare yourself in every way you can by increasing your knowledge and adding to your experience, so that you can make the most of opportunity when it occurs."
—Mario Andretti

"Interruptions can be viewed as sources of irritation or opportunities for service, as moments lost or experience gained, as time wasted or horizons widened. They can annoy us or enrich us, get under our skin or give us a shot in the arm. Monopolize our minutes or spice our schedules, depending on our attitude toward them."
—William Arthur Ward

"Other people's interruptions of your work are relatively insignificant compared with the countless times you interrupt yourself."
—Brendan Francis

"Don't Bother Me Now" May Not Be the Best Response

HAS A DAY ever gone by when you haven't had your share of interruptions? For example, your supervisor makes a surprise visit and hands you another assignment that needs immediate attention. Perhaps a phone call comes to your desk and the conversation draws you into another unexpected workday problem. Maybe a friend stops by and reminds you of something you promised to do for him/her. Suddenly you find yourself attending to work that was unanticipated, and now your best intentions for completing your list of tasks have been thwarted by the unexpected.

I remember when I was in the Novitiate (the period of formation of becoming a nun). There was an easy solution to handling interruptions. That solution was a scheduled life—each moment of the day was determined by the ringing of a bell. This constant clang, which occurred several times a day, reminded us that our lives can be filled with interruptions, but we can always be drawn back to our original task. The bell was just such a reminder of where we were and what we were supposed to be doing. The bell woke us up in the morning, got us to meals and prayer on time, and set the tone for the perfectly planned outline of the day. There were times when the bell was a welcome guest, calling an end to the tedious study period or the arduous manual labor. The bell was also, at times, an unwelcome intrusion. I remember being in the middle of telling a joke to a group of novices, when, just as I reached the dramatic ending, the bell rang. We had to attend immediately to night prayer—and I had to leave everyone hanging until the next morning at breakfast when I was free to deliver the final punch line. Needless to say, the joke was stale by then. The bell was certainly an easy solution to an interrupted life, but it pretty much left us without having to make any personal decisions on our own, which was not so good.

In any case, interruptions can be frustrating because we risk losing track of what we're doing. And, when we rely on our short-term memory, there's a heightened need to get back to that task as soon as possible to avoid forgetting it. However, it's not always possible and often, at the end of a day, we may find ourselves unable to cross anything off of our to-do list, and instead, we have created a longer list for the next day. I guess one could say that "it's all in a day's work." Yes—interruptions can be a source of anxiety and frustration. However, they can also be moments of grace if we are open to welcoming them.

Henri Nouwen, in his book "Out of Solitude" offers this reflection: "A few years ago I met an old professor at the University of Notre Dame. Looking back on his long life of teaching, he said with a funny wrinkle in his eyes: 'I have always been complaining that my work was constantly interrupted, until I slowly discovered that my interruptions were my work.'"[v]

Wow—perhaps that is the great conversion in our lives: to recognize and believe that the many unexpected events in our day are not just disturbing interruptions, but may be surprises that God is gifting us with when we least expect it. The interruptions may be God sending us a present. So—pay close attention to how you respond to interruptions, or to people you consider nuisances because they are bothering you. God may just be the interruption, and then we may be in for a surprise. What if God responded to us in the same way? That would be the real surprise.

CONSIDER THE FOLLOWING

- How can we respond to an interruption with kindness instead of rudeness and insensitivity?

- What do you think this Brendan Francis quote means: "Other people's interruptions of your work are relatively insignificant compared with the countless times you interrupt yourself"?

- In Jesus' life, he saw interruptions as opportunities to display the love of God. Can you think of examples in Scripture that point this out? (Here are a few examples: Mark 5:27-28, Matthew 19:14, Luke 24.)

4

Let Your Yes Mean Yes

"Do not lie to each other, since you have taken off your old self with its practices and have put on the new self, which is being renewed in knowledge in the image of its Creator."
—Colossians 3:9-10 NIV

"Each of you must put off falsehood and speak truthfully to his neighbor, for we are all members of one body."
—Ephesians 4:25 NIV

"The Lord detests lying lips, but he delights in those who tell the truth."
—Proverbs 12:22 NLT

"For the son of God, Jesus Christ, whom we proclaimed among you, Sylvanus and Timothy and I, was not Yes and No, but in him it is always Yes."
—2 Corinthians 1:19 ESV

LATELY I HAVE been partial to the word "maybe." I am always a little hesitant to say yes when it comes to doing something challenging or new, because I am afraid of failing at the project, proposal, or task. I am also a little hesitant to say no because the result is living with the guilt of letting someone down. So, being torn between yes or no often leads me to a "maybe," and the result of the "maybe" can leave someone hanging if I don't follow through with a definite yes or no answer. This new revelation about myself brought me to reflecting this week on the real meaning of the word "yes" and the real meaning of the word "no."

The three important words "Just Say No" became especially popularized during the Reagan administration as words to empower young people and raise awareness of the drug culture. Nancy Reagan went on a powerful campaign to teach children these important words, to give them the courage and power to control their health and their well-being in this world of moral risk.

There are 2,430,000 websites devoted to just saying no. Not only saying no to drugs and alcohol, but also saying no to aqua dots, negativity, religion, surveyors, toxic dump sites, bullying, wasteful spending, etc. I could think of a few more to add to the list —like commercials, political bickering, reality shows, grits, and boring people, just to name a few. There are songs, t-shirts, coffee mugs, and posters all encouraging us to learn these three words and to use them effectively.

There are many articles published claiming to teach us the most effective way to say no. Some state that we don't know how to say no without feeling guilty, so we just need a little practice. Others state that we can still be polite and still smile, but we can also practice saying no while using a polite but assertive tone in our voice.

There are many positive lessons we can learn by just saying no. It can help us in our personal and social life as well as our professional life. Learning how to say no can curb inefficiency, poor management, and mistakes, and thus diminish our level of exhaustion and anxiety. For, if we are too tired and anxious because we have said yes to more than we can handle, this will certainly affect the quality of our work. It's not very kind to ourselves or to the people that we let down.

However, as I try to convince myself that learning how to say no will improve my mental health, I also believe that saying yes might improve my spiritual health. I recently read an article in *Spirituality and Health* magazine entitled "Just Say Yes." This article states that inside of "yes," we all have the capacity to set boundaries. "No" is an essential part of a "yes" way of thinking.[vi]

No, I am unable to do that.

No I don't like the way you are communicating with me.

No, I don't believe that this project is a good idea.

This kind of "no" can lead to "yes." It can lead us to saying yes to our own self-esteem. If we say no to everything, we end up closing ourselves off to new possibilities, new friends, and new opportunities for growth. One great "yes" in history was from Susan B. Anthony, who said, No, women will no longer accept having no rights. Despite having a great fear of public speaking, she stepped into a "yes" state and, with Elizabeth Cady Stanton, traveled throughout the country giving speeches and appealing to the government to treat men and women equally. In 1869, she founded the National Women's Suffrage Association, and went on to say, "Yes, I will vote," in November 1872, for which she was arrested and convicted by a jury that had been instructed by the judge to return a guilty verdict. But her "no" led to "yes" and changed the voting rights of women in this country forever.[vii]

There is also the passage from Matthew 5:37, in which Jesus says, "All you need to say is simply 'Yes' or 'No'; anything beyond this comes from the evil one" (NIV). Perhaps what Jesus is saying is that we need to say what we mean, and mean what we say. Whether we say yes or no, we need to be true to our word. If we are, then those around us will come to trust us when our actions are the same as our words. I think it might also mean that we don't say one thing to one person, and then turn around and say something completely opposite to another.

So, whether we "just say no" or "just say yes," the bottom line is to put aside the mixing of words and equivocation. We need "to keep our word simple, and simply keep our word."

Jesus' words clarified the whole thing for me. I realized then that there probably isn't anything wrong with the words "maybe" or "let me think about it." It is certainly a lot better than saying yes and meaning no, or saying no and meaning yes. What is important is that we are true to our word. We sometimes need to really think of the ramifications of our answer, and our own ability to be true to our commitment.

And, in the end, especially for Christians who work to create a better, kinder universe, the yes and no of our lives boils down to one thing, and one thing only—and that is to tell the truth. For a Christian is a person who loves the truth even though it may sometimes hurt to be truthful.

It's not always easy to tell the truth—but truthfully, it's the honest way to go. "Maybe" there is a lesson here for all of us, just maybe!

CONSIDER THE FOLLOWING

- Have you ever made promises that you were not able to keep? How did it make you feel?

- Have you said yes to people even when you knew that you would not be able to follow through? Were you afraid to say no? What was your reason?

The Side of Kindness

- Are there kind ways to say no and mean ways to say no?

- Was there a time that your "no" was a "yes" to something else?

5

Break the Power of Bad Behavior (Lenten Reflection)

"Anger and bitterness are two noticeable signs of being focused on self and not trusting God's sovereignty in your life. When you believe that God causes all things to work together for good to those who belong to Him and love Him, you can respond to trials with joy instead of anger or bitterness."

—John C. Broger

"Wise anger is like fire from the flint; there is a great ado to bring it out; and when it does come, it is out again immediately."

—Matthew Henry

"Be not angry that you cannot make others as you wish them to be, since you cannot make yourself as you wish to be."

—Thomas à Kempis

"Is all anger sin? No, but some of it is. Even God Himself has righteous anger against sin, injustice, rebellion and pettiness. Anger sometimes serves a useful purpose, so it isn't necessarily always a sin. Obviously, we're going to have adverse feelings, or God wouldn't have needed to provide the fruit of self-control. Just being tempted to do something is not sin. It's when you don't resist the temptation, but do it anyway, that it becomes sin."

—Joyce Meyer

"But the fruit of the Spirit is love, joy, peace, patience, kindness, goodness, faithfulness, gentleness, self-control; against such things there is no law. And those who belong to Christ Jesus have crucified the flesh with its passions and desires. If we live by the Spirit, let us also walk by the Spirit."

—Galatians 5:22-25 ESV

"Be angry and do not sin; do not let the sun go down on your anger, and give no opportunity to the devil. Let the thief no longer steal, but rather let him labor, doing honest work with his own hands, so that he may have something to share with anyone in need."

—Ephesians 4:26-28 ESV

"But now you must put them all away: anger, wrath, malice, slander, and obscene talk from your mouth. […] Put on then, as God's chosen ones, holy and beloved, compassionate hearts, kindness, humility, meekness, and patience, bearing with one another and, if one has a complaint against another, forgiving each other; as the Lord has forgiven you, so you also must forgive."

—Colossians 3:8-13 ESV

DID YOU EVER hear the story of Mike and Mary and their two children? Mary always fixed breakfast for her husband before he went to work. One morning she overslept and quickly got up to fix the breakfast, but because she was rushing she burnt the toast. She called Mike for breakfast. He also overslept and was upset that he had to eat burnt toast for breakfast.

Break the Power of Bad Behavior (Lenten Reflection)

He didn't want to say anything to Mary, but when his son came to the kitchen table he was already upset about the toast, and he took it out on his son. When his son asked for the car keys to go out after school, the father blasted him for asking and said, "Positively no." The son was so angry, but did not want to take it out on his father, so, when his sister came to the table with her homework that she had done the night before, he told her that she had done a terrible job, scribbled all over her paperwork, and stomped out of the room. The daughter sat there crying, but there was no one else in the room to take it out on, so on the way out of the house, she kicked the dog. The dog didn't stop this pattern of behavior, but instead took it out on the poor mailman when he delivered the mail that day, and bit him in the leg. Then the mailman went home and yelled at his wife, and the story goes on and on and on.

Now, relate this story to your own life. When you have experienced anger or resentment, instead of absorbing the pain, letting the pain transform you, or speaking honestly to the person who might have offended you, have you chosen instead to pass it on to the next person you meet? If you are having a bad day, do you often feel that everyone around you better not be having a good one? By golly, you'll change that! Do you pass on the hurt, the pain, and the anger, instead of dealing with it in a positive way?

I can relate this to my own life. Sometimes I carry the hurt for days—it eats my insides out. I pass it on by my silence, sarcasm, or pity parties that I have for myself. Nothing gets done, and this only creates disharmony with those I meet, and disharmony within me.

Sometimes I think that this is what sin is all about— it's the passing on of hurt, anger, or resentment, or playing the victim, or not allowing the hurt to transform me into a better person. Kindness is not related at all to the passing on of hurt, but instead kindness means absorbing it and ending the cycle of negativity.

What better time to make a new resolution than this time of Lent? We normally think of Lent as a time of giving up, so let's first of all give up the passing on of misplaced anger, fear, and resentment. Let's face it squarely where it belongs, and not on the next person you just happen to meet in the hall, or the person with whom you are living or working. This does not mean that people can't help you to carry whatever burden you may have. People are there to help with the pain. We are not meant to carry it by ourselves. But let us learn how to deal with it properly. If someone hurts us, or we are filled with anger at something or someone who treated us unfairly, speak to that person about it, instead of "kicking the dog" or "biting the mailman." Appropriate anger directed to the proper person is healthy, and makes much better sense than not dealing with it and then taking it out on an innocent bystander. Handling conflict, anger, and abusive behavior, to and through the proper channels, will make for a healthier person, inside as well as outside, and it makes for a good Lenten practice as well. We can help recover kindness in our world by stopping the cycle of bitterness and misplaced anger and passing on the courage to handle our problems in an appropriate manner.

CONSIDER THE FOLLOWING

- When you are angry or upset at someone or something, do you find yourself taking it out on someone else? If so, what steps can you follow to change your behavior?

- How can anger serve a useful purpose?

- Have you let the sun go down on your anger? What can you do to avoid going to bed angry?

6

Try Giving Up "Giving Up" This Lent (Lenten Reflection)

"And let us not grow weary of doing good, for in due season we will reap, if we do not give up."
—Galatians 6:9 ESV

"So if there is any encouragement in Christ, any comfort from love, any participation in the Spirit, any affection and sympathy, complete my joy by being of the same mind, having the same love, being in full accord and of one mind. Do nothing from rivalry or conceit, but in humility count others more significant than yourselves. Let each of you look not only to his own interests, but also to the interests of others. Have this mind among yourselves, which is yours in Christ Jesus."
—Philippians 2:1-5 ESV

"If I speak in the tongues of men and of angels, but have not love, I am a noisy gong or a clanging cymbal. And if I have prophetic powers, and understand all mysteries and all knowledge, and if I have all faith, so as to remove mountains, but have not love, I am nothing. If I give away all I have, and if I deliver up my body to be burned, but have not love, I gain nothing. Love is patient and kind; love does not envy or boast; it is not arrogant or rude. It does not insist on its own way; it is not irritable or resentful."

—1 Corinthians 13:1-5 ESV

"Therefore, having this ministry by the mercy of God, we do not lose heart."

—2 Corinthians 4:1 ESV

"Above all, keep loving one another earnestly, since love covers a multitude of sins."

—1 Peter 4:8 ESV

DO YOU REMEMBER your Lenten sacrifices as a child? I remember many during my Catholic school days, especially because Sister Mary Anastasia would remind us constantly of our Lenten observance. And, if we couldn't come up with any serious sins while in her fifth-grade classroom, we could at least offer up our penance for the poor souls in purgatory.

According to Sister Mary Anastasia, though, we were definitely "sinners" in need of repentance. So offer it up we did, and we had to bring in our list of what we were going to give up for Lent and post it on the bulletin board. Then we had to pray that each of our classmates would be faithful to their Lenten sacrifices. After all, we felt pretty bad about the "blood dripping from the wounds of Jesus," so we wanted to be ever so sincere about what we were to give up for Lent.

I remember the two most difficult things I gave up for Lent. The first was the fudgsicles from "Ed's" grocery store. It didn't matter whether it was the middle of summer or winter, a fudgsicle was a fudgsicle—cold, slurpy, downright delicious. Nothing could compare with this chocolate on a stick.

The second thing I gave up for Lent was gossip. For example:

Try Giving Up "Giving Up" This Lent (Lenten Reflection)

"Did you hear that Joey bit Sister Mary Theresa and was expelled from school?"

"Poor Olivia couldn't stop stuttering in Miss Marilyn's class today. It took her double the amount of time to give her oral geography report."

"Did you hear that Patty's hamster got loose in her dad's funeral home and they found it hiding under Mrs. O'Shea's casket?"

I must say that the school playground was pretty miserable for me during Lent. I had to learn to be polite and keep to myself so I wouldn't get involved in talking about my neighbor (B-O-R-I-N-G).

Oh, my—Lent was so hard. I became sufficiently grumpy. When I gave up my favorite foods, my friends began to say to me, "How come when you give up your cookies and fudgsicles, we do the penance?" I guess I made everyone else around me miserable. I bet I didn't win any graces that Lent.

When I think of Lent, I often think of this period of time as a time of sacrifice, penance, and reconciliation. Many people come up with resolutions of what they want to give up.

Do you remember what you gave up as a child? What has changed now? Do you still give up something that was precious to you, or something that you became so attached to that you could not imagine living without, i.e. television, coffee, the phone, etc.?

How about approaching Lent in a different way this year? How about trying to give up giving up? Sounds bizarre, doesn't it? But there are times in life, at least in mine, when I attempted to try to introduce something new, either an idea or a new way of thinking, and it backfires or explodes in my face. There are other times when I decided to speak kindly to someone who previously turned their back on me, only to be ignored again or even bullied in response. Sometimes I find myself just plain tired of trying to get ahead, and instead of taking one step forward, I end up taking ten steps back. If you sense at times a feeling of defeat settling in, or an attitude of "the last page of what's the use," it may be time to try a different tactic.

Let's face it: Lent is not an easy time, but life is not easy, and, I suppose, no one said it would be. So, as we sometimes stumble through the day, wishing that it were a lot easier to get up in the morning, or a lot easier facing the tasks ahead, this Lent maybe our resolution could be... "Don't be a quitter." Don't give up, which can happen all too easily, especially if we are tired, overworked, underpaid, and fresh out of ways to be kind to those who we feel don't deserve good-mannered people like us.

If you want to give up something meaningful this Lent, perhaps you can try to give up "giving up." Please don't give up on yourself—don't give up on being kind, thoughtful, or generous. Don't give up taking the road less traveled; don't give up on trying to change things for the better.

Let's together decide to give up "giving up." After all, Jesus did not give up—and he hasn't given up on us.

CONSIDER THE FOLLOWING

- What will you give up this Lent?

- Have you been giving up lately? What can you do to revive your spirit and not lose heart?

- Are there people in your life who give you hope and encouragement when you feel ready to "give it all up"?

7

O Happy Fault!
(Lenten Reflection)

"When you make a mistake, don't look back at it long. Take the reason of the thing into your mind and then look forward. Mistakes are lessons of wisdom. The past cannot be changed. The future is yet in your power."
—Hugh White (1773-1840)

"Mistakes are the portals of discovery."
—James Joyce

"A man should never be ashamed to own he has been in the wrong, which is but saying ... that he is wiser to-day than he was yesterday."
—Alexander Pope, *Swift's Miscellanies*

LENTEN FRIDAYS WERE very memorable in the convent, especially in the Novitiate, behind closed doors. These Fridays of Lent were set aside as days of recounting one's faults and failings and lining them up during the "Chapter of faults," as it was called back then.

These Fridays were days of penance, when we prepared to confess our faults in the public forum and admit to our community of sisters that we were definitely imperfect. Because, of course, we were, and we were constantly reminded of it in many peculiar ways (of which I dare not go into detail right now!). Whether you broke a dish while in the DWR (dishwashing room) or disobeyed an order from your superior, or forgot to pray your mourning offering (oops, morning offering), you faced the scrutiny of the other postulants and novices and the novice director, and you faced your faults and admitted the error of your ways. Then, you faced a penance, which was usually a strict and scrupulous practice of self-denial. This practice was an immature form of penance, and it was only after Vatican Council II that some of these practices of self-denial were dismissed as a very dysfunctional way of managing and controlling the individual. It was only later that a proper and healthier means of examination of conscience was introduced, and behavior was based more on real virtue rather than indoctrination.

I look back and wonder if I ever really learned from my mistakes when I was in the Novitiate. I grew in fear of making a mistake, of disobeying an order, and often found that I was unable to think for myself. The method used was a fear tactic and often stunted one's growth in maturity and true self-control.

So—it makes me wonder today, how do we learn from our mistakes? In our society today, admitting mistakes is difficult. An implied value in many cultures is that our work represents us: if you fail a test, then you are a failure. If you make a mistake, then you are a mistake.

Stupid and simple mistakes can easily be resolved. Once you recognize the problem and know the better way, you should be able to avoid similar mistakes. Involved mistakes require significant changes to avoid. But, there is a trap. And the trap is refusing to acknowledge our mistakes. Do we know people who have a tendency to brush off their mistakes as not really a mistake, or as a "misstep" caused by someone else? Is this because we don't like to look weak in another person's eyes, and we think that making a mistake is a sign of weakness? If we could only see that the opposite is what is really true —admitting that one did wrong or made a mistake is actually a sign of true strength and willingness to grow as an individual. Is that not the beauty of the sacrament of reconciliation—that one faces oneself as a sinner in need of repentance, and is reminded that truth and forgiveness are at the heart of a Christian life?

So, during the course of the day, in meeting each other and in working together, whether you make a big mistake that stinks up the room, or just a small one that is not a big deal, move on. Admit it, learn from it, and move on. Focus on the improvement aspects and what you can learn from the "error of your ways." And remember: it is always OK to say one of the most important phrases in leadership vocabulary: "I made a mistake."

CONSIDER THE FOLLOWING

- What do you think Hugh White means when he says that "mistakes are lessons of wisdom"?

- How can we learn from our mistakes?

- What kind of changes can we make in order to view our mistakes not as a series of failures, but as learning experiences?

8

Discovering the Beautiful Is Discovering God

"Let the beauty of the Lord our God be upon us."
—Psalm 90:17 KJV

"You will be a crown of splendor in the Lord's hand, a royal diadem in the hand of your God."
—Isaiah 62:3 NIV

"God has chosen to make known among the Gentiles the glorious riches of his mystery, which is Christ in you, the hope of glory."
—Colossians 1:27 NIV

"We, who with unveiled faces all reflect the Lord's glory, are being transformed into his likeness with ever-increasing glory, which comes from the Lord."
—2 Corinthians 3:18 NIV

"Do you not know that your body is a temple of the Holy Spirit within you, whom you have from God?"
—1 Corinthians 6:19 ESV

"I praise you, so wonderfully you made me."
—Psalm 139:14 NAB

If you were asked to describe something beautiful, what would you describe? Would it be a flower from the garden, or a picture of the sunset on the water? Would it be a painting at the art gallery, a glamorous model, a piece of clothing, a newborn baby, a mother and child in each other's embrace? When you think of something beautiful, what picture comes to mind?

It would be an interesting exercise to engage in—that is, to write a list of what you consider beautiful. After you have completed your list of beautiful things, then, check to see if you put yourself on that list. My guess is that you did not. My guess is that a very small percentage of women consider themselves beautiful. It may be higher for men, but not by much.

I decided to write a list of what I considered beautiful. After I completed my list, I decided to take the ultimate beauty quiz that I found online. The directions on this website stated that how you answer the questions will then determine your level of beauty. So I sucked in my breath and my pride, and began the quiz. The beginning questions were not too difficult—define your gender, your age, etc., although I did exaggerate my answers a little when it came to measurements and weight. The rest should have been a breeze, right? Wrong. My first results listed me as markedly similar in looks to a bowl of uncooked dough. Then, when the following question asked me how closely I resembled my dog, I knew I was in trouble—so much for my first and, no doubt, my last beauty quiz.

But it did lead me to wonder how our society really defines beauty, and why we don't think of ourselves as beautiful. After all, we live in a world obsessed with beauty—just search on the web under the words "beauty secrets" and you will find over 43 million websites. Our culture idolizes outward beauty and the people who embody it in our society today. Self-help beautification infomercials often make unbelievable promises—for example, lose fifteen pounds in two weeks with this new exercise formula, try our prepackaged meal for a month and see the results, just ten minutes a day on our machine will give you abs of steel.

"The human soul is hungry for beauty; we seek it everywhere—in landscape, music, art, clothes, furniture, gardening, companionship, love, religion, and in ourselves."[viii] It seems to me that we are constantly in search of beauty. Most of our memories are of beautiful places we have been. And, for a brief time, when in the presence of beauty, we suddenly feel redeemed, free of worry and anxiety. That's how it feels when in the presence of beauty. There is a sense of peace and well-being.

Without realizing it, the word "beauty" and the sense of beauty visits us often during the day. John O'Donohue, in his book "Beauty: The Invisible Embrace," states: "A world without beauty would be unbearable. Beauty is so quietly woven through our ordinary days that we hardly notice it. Everywhere there is tenderness, care and kindness, there is beauty."[ix]

When I think of moments that I remember most, they are usually moments when gazing at something beautiful, when in the presence of uplifting music, or in the presence of landscapes that take your breath away. Those are the moments to remember—a poem that is read to you with such emotion and sense of wonder that you feel you are in the presence of divinity, or moments when someone shares with you their depth of wonder, whether it be of pain or redemption. Those are moments to remember—not moments of fighting in the streets, or people cursing one another, not churches filled with distant people unable to listen to each other's opinions or differing ways of worship. It wasn't landscapes filled with garbage, oil spills in oceans. No, it wasn't any of the above. Instead, it was moments of being in the presence of true beauty. Then, there is inner beauty—which can be the most transformative beauty of all. "If there is beauty in a face it is the soul that lights it up. This beauty comes from within. It is the soul that makes the face beautiful."[x] Beauty calls us forth to "feel its rhythm, to think and act beautifully in the world, to create and live a life that wakens the beautiful."[xi]

Perhaps this week we can make our list of beautiful things, and work toward creating a more beautiful world. Perhaps we can work on moving toward beauty—beauty in each other, and beauty within ourselves. Can you imagine what our life, our home, our work, and our planet would be like if we saw all that God created as beautiful? Perhaps then we would treat each other and those around us not only with incredible awe, but with a level of kindness worthy of incredible respect.

So—let us begin.

First Exercise of the Week:

Think of yourself as beautiful! If this is a difficult practice, there is an easy remedy—pray the passages from Scripture found at the beginning of this chapter as constant reminders this week.

Second Exercise of the Week:

Tell someone that they are beautiful!! Again, this also isn't as hard as it sounds. This doesn't have to be in words such as "Hello, beautiful!" Instead, a kind deed, a look of appreciation, or a word of affirmation and encouragement could certainly help in spreading beauty.

John O'Donohue also states that "in beauty we were dreamed, and created, and offered a life in a world where beauty arises to awaken, surprise, and calls us. Furthermore, whenever we awaken beauty, we are helping to make God present in the world."[xii] So—when we introduce people to beauty, we are introducing them to God.

CONSIDER THE FOLLOWING

- Can you name something beautiful that you saw this week?

- Do you think of yourself as beautiful? Can you think of someone else whom you would describe as beautiful?

- Do you believe that, like Mary, you were immaculately conceived by God, or has there been so much emphasis on original sin that it becomes too difficult to imagine? (Read Ephesians 1:3-5.)

9

Rwanda—A Country of a Thousand Hills and a Thousand Faces of Kindness

"Blood, no matter how little of it, when it spills, spills on the brain, on the memory of a nation."
—Mongane Wally Serote, South African poet

"'Some of the soldiers had come to our house to kill Mum, and my two youngest brothers, but one of the Interahamwe had recognized them and said they should be spared because they had a serving soldier in the family. In a way my brother's rebellion ended up saving their lives. We never saw him again, so we don't really know how the story ends. By 9 p.m. the meal is finally served. Some of the children have fallen asleep next to one another while waiting, in a tangle of limbs, but are roused with the rattle of metal bowls hitting the ground. The boiled bananas look, smell, and taste like potatoes. The peanut soup has become gravy, drizzled on top. Beans are piled high on the side. The children gobble up the meal with hardly a word. Two plastic tubs sit in the corner of the courtyard, one filled with warm soapy water, the other for the rinse. The children eat their fill and bring their metal bowls to the tub to wash. There is no splashing, no arguing, no whining. Instead, they wash their dishes and pile them neatly near the kitchen. They hug Primitiva and disappear into the night. For outsiders it is difficult to square how a country that rage with such violence could find, simultaneously, room for such kindness."

—Dina Temple-Raston, *Justice on the Grass*

AND THE BIRDS STILL SING

Roads untamed

Heat, choking, and
Energy, vanishing.

Tremble of earth and hill, of heart and soul
Torched and troubled.

And the birds still sing.

And everyone walks everywhere
Lame ones, weak ones, little ones,
Strong ones, with their wood and rice, and wheat, and
Coffee beans and banana leaves, and water.
Walking…everywhere…in light…no light. In darkness, no problem.

Babies, hidden under mother and
The endless chant
OF
JAMAIS ENCORE!!
NEVER AGAIN!!

In this country of a thousand hills, and
The people say
A thousand problems – where the labor is
Endless
One carries water, and other people's lives.

And the birds still sing.

And vegetation still rises from the earth, along with hope and forgiveness.

And the flowers still bloom
And the children still play
And the mother still give birth
And the plants still grow, and the people still infirm,
And life still goes on – in shacks, in huts, and sheds and
Forests, and in one's soul.

And, for me…there lies the mystery.

How, Why…do the birds still sing?
—Sandra Makowski

Background

The country of Rwanda has a special place in the thoughts and the hearts of the Sisters of St. Mary. The Sisters opened their first mission in Rwanda, fifty years ago at the time of this writing. At that time, Rwanda was a colony of Belgium.

Before 1994, most people were unaware of the country of Rwanda. It rests as a dot on the map of Africa, nestled between the larger, more visible countries such as Tanzania, Uganda, and the Democratic Republic of Congo. Rwanda is a country smaller than the state of Maryland, yet is one of the most densely populated African countries. It covers a region of mountains, high plateaus, and savannas. It is a country with a troubled history, including colonization by Germany and Belgium, civil wars, political coups, and wars with neighboring countries. But nothing could have prepared it for the genocide that took place in April of 1994. On the sixth of April, the airplane carrying Rwandan President Habvyarimana, along with the president of Burundi, was shot down as it prepared to land at Kigali airport. Both presidents died when the plane crashed. Responsibility for the attack is disputed, with the extremists of both ethnic groups (Tutsi and Hutu) being blamed. In spite of disagreements about the identity of the perpetrators, the attack on the plane is, to many observers, the catalyst for the genocide.

Thus began one hundred days of killings, with as many as one million people slaughtered at the hands of fellow Rwandans. Most of the victims were killed in their own villages or in towns, often by their neighbors and fellow villagers. Militia members typically murdered their victims by hacking them with machetes, although some army units used rifles. Victims were often found hiding in churches and school buildings, where Hutu gangs massacred them. Ordinary citizens were called on by local officials and the government-sponsored radio to kill their neighbors, and those who refused to kill were often murdered themselves. One such massacre occurred at Nyarabuye, where 1,500 Tutsis sought refuge in their Catholic church. However, the killers then used bulldozers to knock down the church buildings, and everyone was killed. When the hundred days were over, it is estimated that as many as one million people had been slaughtered.

This was in 1994, and many things have happened since then. But this certainly has changed the country forever. In 2004 and 2005, President Paul Kagame attempted to restore peace, equality, and stabilization in the country. Rwanda's decision to cut off its relationship with France and its desire to join the African Congress (which is made up of English-speaking nations) began to transform the country from a French-speaking country into an English-speaking country. This has certainly proved to be challenging for the Sisters of St. Mary, who now, fifty years after their arrival in the country, have over forty Rwandan Sisters working and ministering to the people.

It was this change in the country's national language that led me to take a leave of absence from my work in South Carolina and spend two months with our Rwandan Sisters to help teach English.

Finding Kindness in the Hills

I have a treasure chest of memories related to a brief period of time I spent in Rwanda, in the year 2009, helping to teach English to our Sisters. The most remarkable memories are those of faces: faces of children, strangers, and the Sisters. I have quite a few pictures of the orphan children of Ruyenzi—some of them taken when they were in their afternoon nap poses, gazing up at me with wide, expectant, tired, wary eyes. Then there were the eyes of Jeremie and Benoit, the three-year-old twins who followed me everywhere, often running down the hill toward me with their little arms wide open, wanting to receive a mother's embrace. I wanted so badly to hide them in my suitcase and take them home with me.

I remember the faces of the crippled and hungry, waiting at the house for food or drink on Good Friday. Their faces showed fatigue and longing as they waited at the house, one man with only one leg, and a woman with her hungry baby.

I remember the faces of the Sisters—their anguish at not being able to do more or be more, in a land full of heavy sorrow, and these same faces breaking down in incredible laughter at a funny word or a funny-sounding new English phrase, or beaming with accomplishment when they could recite the days of the week, or the months of the year, in English, without sputtering or tripping over the "th-" words. I remember the laughter of Soeur Marie Camille, which was so incredibly infectious that you would laugh without any reason except that her laughter made you laugh. I remember her laughing when she would say, "I am pleased to meet you too." With the heavy accent on "too," then the look of absolute pride because of her great accomplishment.

I remember the face of Soeur Jeanne d'Arc who, at times, would simply stare during English class. You knew she was not there—she was somewhere else, and you hated to think of what she saw or where she was in her memory.

I remember the face of Febronie, who sometimes showed fear or hesitation, and then, out of nowhere, would appear with laughing eyes and say "No problem" even when she was throwing up in the back seat of the van during the winding, harrowing, adventurous and long, long, long ride to Nyungwe National Forest. (I can still remember Soeur Marie Camille saying that it was just a two-hour drive—and reminding her of that five hours later.)

I remember the faces of those in church during the genocide memorial. There were many faces that I could not read: many looked sad and worn, torched or troubled. I found faces that held more than sorrow, and I found faces of strength and hope.

But the faces that I loved most were the faces of the Sisters with whom I lived and met during my brief stay. I felt that they were truly my sisters—these foreigners whom I had never met were really not foreigners at all, nor strangers. They were my sisters— those whom I had loved all of these years, but had never met. Is that what real, extraordinary kindness is—when one is loved by strangers who turn out to be saints? They were faces of courage, generosity, and most of all, kindness. They loved and cared for me, even during the disastrous stations of the cross which I attempted to walk, during my dismal attempts at speaking French, during a few depressing moments when all I heard was Kinyarwanda, during the times when I looked lost or forlorn, and they took the time to walk me along the route to my room so that I would not fall, always making sure I had enough to eat, and even making me a chocolate cake.

I have made many mistakes and made some poor choices and decisions in my life —and, hopefully, I've learned some powerful lessons throughout this journey that I call my life. But making the decision to go to Rwanda has, without doubt, been one of the best decisions I have ever made. Thank you, Sisters, one and all—thank you.

CONSIDER THE FOLLOWING

- Is there someone in your life you have been unable to forgive? Why? What can you do to change your inability to forgive? Have you prayed for the grace to be able to forgive?

- Did you ever find yourself accusing someone of something that you later discovered they did not do? How did you handle this?

- What does Jesus tell us about forgiveness? Spend some time with the passages in the Bible that speak of forgiveness (e.g. Matthew 5:17; Matthew 6:12; Matthew 6: 14-15; Matthew 26:26-28).

- How can a moment of reconciliation become a moment of transformation?

- In what ways could you help create a culture of forgiveness in your family, workplace, or church?

10

What Do You Want to Be? How About a Saint?

"To the church of God which is at Corinth, to those who have been sanctified in Christ Jesus, saints by calling, with all who in every place call on the name of our Lord Jesus Christ, their Lord and ours."
—1 Corinthians 1:2 NASB

"We are all called to Christian perfection, 'all the faithful, whatever their condition or state, are called by the Lord, each in his own way, to that perfect holiness whereby the Father Himself is perfect.'"
—The Second Vatican Council, *Lumen Gentium* (11.3)

"Charity is the soul of the holiness to which all are called; it governs, shapes, and perfects all the means of sanctification."
—The Catechism of the Catholic Church (826)

When I was a young child, still in grade school, I used to imagine what it would be like to live in the beautiful house across the street. It was white with white pillars and a very big yard. I never saw anyone going in or out of this house, but it was so different from all of the other houses in the neighborhood, almost as if it had landed there from another time and place in history. I used to imagine myself as the mistress of the "beautiful house." I would get all dressed up in high heels and a long flowing gown. I would have a closet full of mink coats, and maids running all over the place being paid just to make me happy. I would ring the bell for the butler, and I could watch *Gunsmoke* all day on television if I wanted to. What did I want to be when I grew up? I wanted to be the rich lady in the beautiful house across the street. But then, when I used to get all involved in the westerns on television, I also imagined myself as Annie Oakley. I would ride my horse across the Wild West, put the bad guys in jail, and go about bringing peace to the planet. What a great life it would be. I guess every other week, depending on what television program I was watching, or who I met, I would change my mind as to what I wanted to be when I grew up—each week I introduced myself to an adventure even more dramatic than the week before.

Do you think back on those days when you could imagine a different life, a kind of fantasy life, where you just could enter the world of pretend and become an imaginary hero, saving the world and doing good, or just being rich and having everything you ever wanted?

I don't ask myself the question "What do I want to be when I grow up?" anymore, but now I ask the question, "Who do I want to be?" It's never too late to ask that question, and it's never too late to imagine the answer. And, as I get older, that seems to be the more important question. The church places a lot of emphasis on the fact that we are all sinners, in continual need of repentance. Another possibility for us, however, would be to concentrate on our call to sainthood. I suppose there is no doubt that we are sinners—but there also should be no doubt that we have the possibility, too, of becoming saints.

Who is a saint? I guess there are many ways in which one could describe a saint. One could say that a saint is someone who has demonstrated heroic virtue, or someone who is a friend of God—someone who is in heaven. Paul says in Galatians 2:19-21, "I live, yet, no longer I, but Christ lives in me." Each of the saints had human flaws and faults, but my guess is that they never stopped in their search for holiness. That, perhaps, is what makes them saints.

In her book *Saint-Watching,* Phyllis McGinley writes that saints are human beings with an added dimension. "They are obsessed by goodness and by God as Michelangelo was obsessed by line and form, as Shakespeare was bewitched by language, Beethoven by sound."[xiii] She also states that, although saints may be different in many ways, they are always generous. "You will never find a stingy saint."[xiv]

Saints were not perfect—they were flawed individuals filled with doubts. But, they were friends of God—they lived a life of prayer and were gifted with selflessness and holiness.

I am sure that we all have our favorite saints. Perhaps we were named after a saint, or our Confirmation name was taken after we studied the life of a particular saint. There are perhaps certain saints we pray to, and we ask intercession from them. St. Anthony was always a good example. We may remember the prayer rhyme to him, "Tony, Tony, look around, something's lost that must be found." He was the saint we would pray to, to help us find something we had lost. And how about St. Jude, the saint for impossible causes? I prayed to him a lot.

Some of the saints had it tough—especially when thinking about those who died a martyred death. I think of St. Joan of Arc who was burned alive, or the torture of some of the North American martyrs.

Saints were not perfect—it is told that St. Jerome had a terrible temper, and that people were just as happy when St. Aloysius was not around, since he seemed like such a morbid person. So, what did they have that made it possible for them to be declared a saint by the church? Saints were not born saints, and they weren't born with haloes around their heads, and they didn't glow in the dark. It's just that they never gave up and never stopped trying to be and to do better.

Could we say that saints were kind people? My guess is that kindness became their constant companion. It is what they carried with them when they prayed, when they worked for justice, and when they were martyred for the sake of the gospel. It became their companion in their life of prayer and the gifts that they developed in the service of others. It was with them when they developed a life of prayer, and it was what they developed as a special project—to imitate the Master.

So, in answer to the question "Who do I want to be when I grow up?" do I want to be a kind person? Do I want to carry kindness as my constant companion? Do I, then, want to be a saint? Yes, I want to be holy. Oh, sure, maybe we want to be rich, or successful, or happy, or popular. But in the end, what is really important? How about being a saint? Can I just as well strive for that goal too? There are a splendid variety of saints, and I can answer the call to be one of them, with the great cloud of witnesses—I can be that person who hears the word of God and responds to the call to be holy. Each of the saints was called, and each answered the call in a different way. I can be one of those people.

CONSIDER THE FOLLOWING

- Do you have a favorite saint? Why did you choose this person? What do you admire most about this saint?

- What qualities do you think are the most important in becoming a saint?

- What can you do in your own life to strive toward holiness and to be an inspiration to others?

11

Give Yourself the Gift of Patience (Holiday Kindness)

"Do not fear, for I am with you; do not anxiously look about you, for I am your God. I will strengthen you, surely I will help you, surely I will uphold you with My righteous right hand."
—Isaiah 41:10 NASB

"Praise be to the God and Father of our Lord Jesus Christ, the Father of compassion and the God of all comfort, who comforts us in all our troubles, so that we can comfort those in any trouble with the comfort we ourselves receive from God."
—2 Corinthians 1:3-4 NIV

"And God shall wipe away all tears from their eyes; and there shall be no more death, neither sorrow, nor crying, neither shall there be any more pain: for the former things are passed away."
—Revelation 21:4 KJV

> "Come to Me, all who are weary and heavy-laden, and I will give you rest."
> —Matthew 11:28 NASB

It is difficult to ignore the fact that at Christmas, Easter, Thanksgiving, or any time approaching a holiday, the thought of loved ones who have passed on will be uppermost in your mind. As much as you try to put on a happy face when meeting your friends or relatives for the holiday dinner or the festive plans, your mind is consumed with those whom you love and who are no longer with you. You can even see them in your room, or sitting in the background watching you. Yet, you can't say anything to your guests, who will think that you have lost your mind. So you sit and pretend that you are really enjoying yourself during these holiday preparations, and you pretend that all is okay, when it really isn't.

Grieving is a part of the holiday stressors. You can't help but think of your loved ones who have died. Not that you don't think of them every day already, but holidays are different. Holidays, especially Christmas, are advertised on television, radio, store ads, churches, and workplaces, as a time when family is together. Expectations are so incredibly high that the letdown becomes that much more painful.

What can we do to handle this kind of grief, which comes intruding on our desire to enjoy this festive season?

One way to handle it is to lower our expectations. No family is perfect and no household is without its own problems and stressors during the holidays. No holiday will be without its nostalgia, its sense of loss, and its imperfections. So—lower the bar, and just accept the fact that you *will* feel lonesome, you *will* miss loved ones who have passed on. Don't deny your true feelings. Once you can expect to feel grief, and know that it is normal, then it feels better already.

Give Yourself the Gift of Patience (Holiday Kindness)

The second way to handle this kind of stress during the holidays is to acknowledge the empty chair. Sometimes families can do a little dance—like, "Do we want to talk about him or her?" or "Should we just ignore the fact and hope the feeling will go away?" It is suggested by some counselors that acknowledging the person with a physical space, like a photo or a candle, is helpful. I also think that at a special time, perhaps at the grace before meals, a special prayer could be added, to indicate that of course this particular person is on your mind. This can help you to admit it and own it, in a sense. And then acknowledge the fact that life can go forward if we let it.

I remember my first Christmas without my mom, when I decided to help serve Christmas dinner at Neighborhood House, a community center that feeds and clothes the homeless. I felt drawn to Jacob, who was a regular at Neighborhood House. I pegged him as a poor, hopeless soul who I was going to help make his holiday happier. I would plaster him with my pious platitudes and make him feel better. Guess what? I soon discovered that he was a computer genius, he read about three books a day—and he had lost his wife and children in a car accident. He never survived this tragedy. He began drinking. He lost his job, his house, and his life as he knew it. After meeting him, I knew that other people grieve in a way that I never could imagine. It was then that I began to heal. I didn't help him; he helped me that year. He reached out to me in the telling of his story. But he did not survive his grief. I can survive the grief and my life can go on. The person you are grieving wouldn't want it any other way.

So—another way to handle the stress of the holidays is, certainly, to have patience with yourself. It's all right to feel lonely; it's okay to miss someone you love. But, also allow others to change you, allow others to help you, and allow yourself the opportunity to reach out to others. Be especially kind to those who grieve during this time.

And accept the kindness of others. Then you will soon discover that we are all one in some form or other. We are all connected—we will soon discover the art of compassion, and that can be the most honest and most rewarding moment of the holiday season.

CONSIDER THE FOLLOWING

- Do you find it difficult to accept the kindness of others? Why is that? What can you do to be more accepting of other people's acts of kindness?

- Do you understand the stages of grief? Does it help you to be more patient with yourself and more tolerant of others' pain during times of grief?

- Do you have a favorite Scripture passage that offers you hope and consolation during times of grieving and/or during the holiday time?

12

The Art of Listening— We Have Two Ears and One Mouth for a Reason

"Then you will call on me and come and pray to me, and I will listen to you."
—Jeremiah 29:12 NIV

"And He was saying, "He who has ears to hear, let him hear."
—Mark 4:9 NASB

"Then the Lord came and stood and called as at other times, "Samuel, Samuel! And Samuel said, "Speak, for Your servant is listening."
—1 Samuel 3:10 NASB

"But prove yourselves doers of the word, and not merely hearers who delude themselves."
—James 1:22 NASB

The Side of Kindness

Story Number One

Okay—so I'm at the doctor's office; I go up to the counter to check in at the desk. After waiting for the receptionist to finish her phone conversation, I give her my name and tell her I am there for my appointment. Her eyes stay focused on her computer. She checks my status and then says to me, "Now, the last time you were here, you had dislocated your shoulder, is that correct?" I give a little frown, knowing she has me mixed up with someone else. "No," I say, "that wasn't me, since this is my first visit here." She doesn't blink an eye and continues to look at the computer screen. Then she says, "And your primary language is Russian?" Now I am really wondering who she has me confused with, but again, I tell her that she is again incorrect—my primary language is not Russian. I say to myself, I've been speaking English with her since I went up to her desk. She still never looks up from the computer screen, almost as if I am not there. I really am not sure that she has heard me at all. I continue to stand there, befuddled, wondering if I should go out the door and come in again, until she says to me, "Okay, please take a seat, Dr. Smith will be with you momentarily." Then I turn completely blank and find myself saying, "Okay—who is Dr. Smith?" She then says to me, "Dr. Smith is your primary care doctor. That's who you're here to see, right?" (She says this as if I am the crazy one.) "No," I say, "I never heard of Dr. Smith." It is at that moment that she takes her eyes off the computer and looks at me for the first time. Finally... finally... I think I got her attention.

Story Number Two

A patient is exiting a health care facility. The desk attendant can tell that she is a bit uneasy, maybe even a bit dissatisfied. "Did everything go all right with the procedure?" the clerk asks. "Mostly," the patient replies.

(If there is ever a hint that something was wrong, the term "mostly" has to be it.) "Good," the clerk abruptly responds, and then follows with a resounding "Next!"

Story Number Three

A coworker is in your office talking to you about the statistical plan for a new building, and you never hear a word she says because your mind is somewhere else. Suddenly she asks you a question about something she has just said, and you cannot answer because you have been pretending to listen for the past fifteen minutes. You had completely zoned out.

Now, the question is, what do these three stories have in common? Answer: They are all stories about listening.

Listening is not the same as hearing. Listening and hearing are two very distinct actions. Hearing is the act of receiving a sound. You can close your eyes to avoid seeing, you can pinch your nose to avoid smelling, you can shrink away to avoid being touched, but your ears have no flaps to cover them. Their structure suggests that for your own protection, your ears should never be closed, even when you sleep. Because you cannot close your ears, you receive and hear sounds constantly. But listening is much more than hearing. Listening is a skill, and just because a person is speaking does not necessarily mean that they are being listened to. Listening is often hard work. It requires us to give another person our attention. And knowing how to listen well is a good part of being kind. Listening is clearly an essential skill for effective communication, and the best way to improve our listening skills is to practice. One way that we can practice the art of listening (because it is an art) is to place ourselves in the other person's shoes. We can try to enter the conversation from the other person's perspective. It would not be a good idea to consider ourselves smarter than the other person, or to think that we already know what they are going to say.

We can also practice by praying for the grace of a listening heart, because listening requires not only good ears but a listening heart. We have plenty of examples of that in the Scriptures. In fact, the word "heart" is found in the Scriptures 743 times. We can read about the prophets who continually urge people to listen. So perhaps we can try to do a little more "listen" and a little less "talk." Remember, we have two ears and one mouth for a reason.

CONSIDER THE FOLLOWING

- What are some tell-tale signs that indicate a person is not really listening?

- How can we develop a listening heart?

- What is the difference between listening and hearing? What are the qualities of a good listener?

13

Knowing How to Fail May Lead You to Success

"For a righteous man falls seven times, and rises again, but the wicked stumble in time of calamity."
—Proverbs 24:16 NASB

"You shall say to them, 'Thus says the Lord, "Do men fall and not get up again? Does one turn away and not repent?'"
—Jeremiah 8:4 NASB

"By grace you have been saved through faith; and that not of yourselves, it is the gift of God; not as a result of works, so that no one may boast."
—Ephesians 2:8-9 NASB

"If at first you don't succeed, try, try again. Then quit. There's no point in being a damn fool about it."
—W.C. Fields

"Only those who dare to fail greatly can ever achieve greatly."
—Senator Robert F. Kennedy

The Side of Kindness

I suppose, if I had to, I could start keeping a list of episodes in my life where I failed. For example, I remember failing my first driving test—what an embarrassment. It wasn't like I was just seventeen at the time. I was twenty-seven years old. This was humiliating enough that it took me a while to try again.

I remember, when I was a novice, I was chosen to spend a year in our international Novitiate in Belgium. It was an honor to be chosen to represent our American Province. I was to go for a period of two years—I lasted one. Why? Because after one year, I begged Mother Superior to send me home. I was so lonesome, so lost, could not speak the language, and questioned everything (which is not what novices do...). I was then told I was a very disobedient novice and would probably never make it to final vows. I was sent home in shame.

I remember spending two months in a remote part of Rwanda. I went to teach English to our Rwandan Sisters. I wanted desperately to participate in the village's memorial of the genocide, which was a procession up one side of a mountain and down the other side while chanting the psalms. This was to take place on Good Friday. Little did I understand that this journey was at least a ten-hour journey on foot. I couldn't make it. I had to stop halfway up the mountain and rest. I was too tired, too hungry, and with two swollen feet I could not continue. I rested on the side of the mountain until a villager with a motorbike picked me up and took me back home. No one said I was a failure—in fact, they were filled with sympathy—but, I sure felt like one.

I remember working in an office and being told that I could not follow directions, was disobedient to rules, incompetent, and unreliable, and would never succeed. I was close to quitting or being fired, whichever came first. Fortunately, I was saved by the mysterious hand of God.

The list of failures could go on, but you probably get the point, and, if you want, you can make a list of your own failures—the times in your life when you remember failing miserably at something you did, or something you didn't do. Life is filled with them. What matters, however, is not that you failed, but how and what you learned from it. I know that I learned resilience. Resilience means being able to adapt to life's misfortunes and setbacks. When you have resilience, you harness inner strength that helps you rebound from a setback or challenge, such as a job loss or a job difficulty, an illness, a disaster, or the death of a loved one. If you lack resilience, you might dwell on problems, feel victimized, or just plain give up.

Or—another alternative—you can begin to make a list of people in history who were labeled failures and became successful because of their resilience. For example, Leo Tolstoy flunked out of college. He was described as both "unable and unwilling to learn."[xv] Henry Ford went broke and failed five times before he succeeded.[xvi] When Lucille Ball began studying to be an actress in 1927, she was told by the head instructor of the John Murray Anderson Drama School to "try any other profession."[xvii] Walt Disney was fired by a newspaper editor because "he lacked imagination and had no good ideas."[xviii]

The list goes on with such people as Abraham Lincoln, Socrates, Louisa May Alcott, Emily Dickinson, Vincent van Gogh, and Thomas Edison. Thomas Edison's teachers said he was "too stupid to learn anything." He was fired from his first two jobs for being nonproductive. As an inventor, Edison made 1,000 unsuccessful attempts at inventing light bulbs. When a reporter asked, "How did it feel to fail 1,000 times?" Edison replied," I didn't fail 1,000 times. The light bulb was an invention with 1,000 steps."[xix]

So—do we interpret failure as the end of a task, hopefully to never be repeated? Or, do we look upon failure as a learning experience, as part of life and part of the story of who we are—not a failure, but someone who continually succeeds because we grasped life at its fullest and learned something from it? We become someone who does not give up, but grows up, with more wisdom, and flourishes more than ever before. If we just sat on our rump and decided not to try anything new because we were afraid of making a mistake, or of failing in the task, then we would be getting nowhere in life.

The moral of the story then comes from a quote from Confucius that says, "Our greatest glory is not in never failing but in rising every time we do."[xx] And, of course, isn't our faith based on the fact that death did not have the last word? Doesn't our faith celebrate the fact that what masqueraded as failure becomes the ultimate success—the resurrection of Christ? Alleluia, Alleluia.

CONSIDER THE FOLLOWING

- What does it mean that "knowing how to fail may lead you to success"? Is there a right way and a wrong way to fail?

- Have you ever failed in something and it turned out for the best? Was a new path opened up for you?

- Have you ever been called a failure? How did it make you feel? Did you give in to it, or did you go on to prove that person wrong?

14

Believe in the Impossible

"Faith expects from God what is beyond all expectation."
—Andrew Murray

"Faith makes all things possible ... love makes all things easy."
—D.L. Moody

"Faith, mighty faith, the promise sees, And looks to God alone; Laughs at impossibilities, And cries it shall be done."
—Charles Wesley

"To learn strong faith is to endure great trials. I have learned my faith by standing firm amid severe testing."
—George Mueller

"The report of this came to the ears of the church in Jerusalem, and they sent Barnabas to Antioch. When he came and saw the grace of God, he was glad, and he exhorted them all to remain faithful to the Lord with steadfast purpose, for he was a good man, full of the Holy

Spirit and of faith. And a great many people were added to the Lord."
—Acts 11:22-24 ESV

"And if I have prophetic powers, and understand all mysteries and all knowledge, and if I have all faith, so as to remove mountains, but have not love, I am nothing."
—1 Corinthians 13:2 ESV

"So we are always of good courage. We know that while we are at home in the body we are away from the Lord, for we walk by faith, not by sight."
—2 Corinthians 5:6-7 ESV

Sometimes God's kingdom seems like an impossible dream. We look around and we see enmity between countries and peoples, the weary faces of refugees fleeing their homelands, the hollow eyes of hungry children. We witness violence in our streets, neighbor against neighbor. We even see it in people who call themselves Christian, who condemn others and one another because of differences in belief or philosophy. Yes, God's kingdom seems like an impossible dream. It takes a lot of faith to look around this world of ours and see God's kingdom.

We feel like Alice in Wonderland when she told the Queen of Hearts, "One can't believe impossible things."

"I daresay that you haven't had much practice," said the Queen. "When I was your age, I always did it for half-an-hour a day. Why, sometimes I've believed as many as six impossible things before breakfast."[xxi]

Christian belief begins with the impossible—rising from the dead—and goes on to dream of such things as abolishing hatred, ending wars, and banishing racial prejudice.

Look at your own inability to forgive someone, and dream of embracing that person. Reach out to someone at work, perhaps someone you have been avoiding, and do something special for that person. If there is someone with whom you have some tension, take the first step and try to remedy it. It is, as the Queen observed, just a matter of practice—or, as Jesus would have it, a matter of faith.

Think of all the things that you have accomplished so far in your life—and now think about how many of them you thought were impossible tasks. How many tragedies have you endured and thought you would never survive them—the grief, the sleepless nights, the tear-filled days, watching and waiting for loved ones to go home to God? Have you had the experience of grieving the loss of a loved one and being convinced that you would never experience happiness again, since you thought it impossible to actually survive the grief? You have, no doubt, survived many things despite impossible odds. You have been kind to people you never thought deserving, and others have been kind to you despite the fact that you didn't think they had it in them to be kind. Think of bread and wine becoming body and blood—think of death not having the last word.

We are asked by our faith to stake our life on what, by some, are considered impossible tasks, and we are called, sometimes, to practice the impossible—to believe in God's promise of Jesus Christ, one born among us who lives in our midst for all time. Peace is possible. Living without hunger and famine is possible. The glory of God can be found everywhere and in everyone. God's demands are possible, but require faith and practice, dreaming and working together. Together we can work to help build a better world, if we but believe that God can do the impossible—and, if God is with us, who can be against us? Let us consider the dream and embrace the task ahead.

CONSIDER THE FOLLOWING

- Were you ever asked to do something that you thought was an impossible task? What happened in the end?

- Have you ever put your trust in what seemed like an impossible goal? What "impossible" things have you accomplished?

- Have you been able to forgive someone or been able to mend a relationship that you thought could never be repaired?

- Have you ever expressed kindness toward an individual whom you thought you could never forgive, or someone who had been particularly mean to you?

15

You Don't Need a Pedometer to Make Every Step Count

"The one who says he abides in Him ought himself to walk in the same manner as He walked."
—1 John 2:6 NASB

"Therefore be careful how you walk, not as unwise men but as wise, making the most of your time, because the days are evil. So then do not be foolish, but understand what the will of the Lord is."
—Ephesians 5:15-17 NASB

"He has shown you, O mortal, what is good. And what does the Lord require of you? To act justly and to love mercy and to walk humbly with your God."
—Micah 6:8 NIV

I bought a pedometer last month so that I could keep track of my steps as I walk. It's been said by many a fitness expert, as well as medical doctors, that walking can help pave the way to fitness. Using a pedometer can help one to set and achieve goals for better health. So, I thought that if I bought a pedometer and aimed for

10,000 steps a day, my motivation would improve and I could walk myself towards better health. So—off I went, pedometer hooked to my belt, headphones in place, ready with my walking tape and my new Nike shoes, and out the door I went. Thirty minutes and three thousand steps later, I was finished with that part of my exercise, with only 7,000 steps to go. However, I soon realized that, during my walk, I didn't even take notice of the fish in the lake or the alligator that has recently been snooping ever so close to shore. I also paid little attention to the new flowers that had just been planted outside my window. I didn't hear the meow from the cat that was following me, nor did I hear the roar of the engine from the car that nearly drove me off the sidewalk when turning into the driveway. I was completely unaware of my surroundings, since I was so conscious of "just getting it done." That's when I began to recall those times when walking wasn't something that you had to build into your schedule as an extra chore. It was what you did, part of who you were. Then I began to think of what I had been missing in my daily walks, and that is…awareness. I began to think of all the other walks that have been etched in my memory, not as a fitness regimen, but as a reminder of the melody of life, before life lost its melody.

    I remember the walk to and from school every day. I grew up in an area where there was no school bus, and we had no money for a city bus. So we set off, my sister and I. We would smile and wave at our neighbors sitting on their front porches. We played the hopscotch game when we passed the sidewalks still outlined with chalk where we used to play until dark. Then, when we saw the dog running after the postman, we would run after the dog, seeing who could get to the postman first. Our last stop on the way to school was on the bridge, where we paused to see if we could catch a tadpole and hide it in our pockets so we could set it loose in the classroom and see what Sister Mary Anastasia would do. This was walking—this was a melody of my life, played over and over, in playfulness and abandon. This was a time and a place when, during those forty-five minutes to and from school, I had not a care in the world. I abandoned myself to the journey and took in the sights and sounds, and all else of worry and fear was left behind.

After entering the convent, we had one special day a week when we were free from our afternoon chores in the bake room, the laundry room, the dishwashing room, and the kitchen. It was the same day that we had Freddie's donuts delivered for breakfast. That day we could relax from our daily schedule and go for a walk to the cemetery. To the casual observer, this certainly sounds bizarre—that we would be looking forward to walking to the cemetery. However, we could leave the convent walls for a couple of hours, walk down Delaware Avenue, smell the apples on the apple trees, walk amidst the flat grave markers marked with familiar names like Sister Mary Liquori, Stanislaus, and Gonzaga, and the memories of what they must have been like. We would breathe in the breath of the spirits surrounding those flat graves, with names of people we had never met, but had heard of their holiness and seen it in the works that they had accomplished and that we so humbly were asked to continue. We looked forward to these weekly walks. There we were, in full habit, walking two by two, chattering like small schoolchildren after dismissal, until we reached the flat markers with names of holiness, and then we walked in silence and awe. These are walks that have been etched in my memory. This was also one of the melodies of my life.

There are many more memories of walks—walks in the hills of Rwanda, walking the same hills and forests where people hid from machete-fighting enemies who at one time were neighbors and friends. Rwanda—a country where everyone walks: lame ones, weak ones, little ones, strong ones, with their wood and rice, and wheat and coffee beans and banana leaves and water, walking everywhere, remembering each step as part of the melody of suffering, when forgetting might have been better.

Today there seems to be an emphasis on walking for better physical health. But there was a time when walking was a time to take in the view, to be aware of what was around you, and what you were around. It could be the way of the happy wanderer or the way of the cross. Either way, it was a melody of life played out in each step. Now, we walk to count our steps, we walk while we text, we walk while we talk on our cell phones, we walk with the sound of music, or something called music, in our ears. We walk to get someplace, not to be in someplace.

Life is too short not to live it in the moments we have. We all have very busy schedules—we work all day, and we work hard at what we do. We often don't have time for the moment we are in, since we are planning some future event, or meeting a crisis that takes us beyond the moment. The time then is lost in deadlines and details. So, every once in a while, let's give ourselves a present—the present. Let us learn not to take a walk, but to give ourselves to a walk, where we can be present to the present, breathe the air, and listen to the sounds that surround our being. The mystery of the moment is that it opens all moments. If we can give ourselves to the moment during our daily walk, perhaps we can also make every step count, not only in the walk, but in the moments of our daily life.

CONSIDER THE FOLLOWING

- What does it mean to "give yourself to a walk" instead of to "take a walk"?

- How can we learn to live in the present moment, and see it as a gift?

- How is time lost in the deadlines and details? What can we do to "enjoy the journey"?

16

Kindness— and a Canon Law Degree

"The Lord is my light and my salvation; whom shall I fear? The Lord is the defense of my life; whom shall I dread? When evildoers came upon me to devour my flesh, my adversaries and my enemies, they stumbled and fell. Though a host encamp against me, my heart will not fear; though wars arise against me, in spite of this I shall be confident."

—Psalm 27:1-3 NASB

"Fear thou not; for I *am* with thee: be not dismayed; for I *am* thy God: I will strengthen thee; yea, I will help thee; yea, I will uphold thee with the right hand of my righteousness."

—Isaiah 41:10 KJV

"For God hath not given us the spirit of fear; but of power, and of love, and of a sound mind."

—2 Timothy 1:7 KJV

"Humble yourselves therefore under the mighty hand of God, that he may exalt you in due time: Casting all your care upon him; for he careth for you."
—1 Peter 5:6-7 KJV

How and why I ever became interested in canon law is a story all its own. But the Sisters of St. Mary of Namur have always exemplified, for me, a true pioneer spirit. That same spirit that possessed the Sisters of St. Mary possessed me as well. Working in canon law may not sound very "pioneerish" to some people. However, women had not been allowed in the canon law program until the 1983 Code of Canon Law took effect. So in 1987, when, for the first time, the Buffalo, New York diocese opened a tribunal judge position to a woman, I applied for the job. I stepped into the interview room all dressed up in my grey pinstriped suit, my serious-looking glasses resting perfectly on my nose, my community cross hanging around my neck, and a facial stare which was a poor attempt on my part to imitate ecclesiastical confidence. As bad as I looked, it worked. I was accepted for the position.

My agreement with the diocese was that I was to commit to at least a five-year term. Before the term began, I would be required to attend Catholic University and enter the canon law program, which the diocese would finance. The two years in school were a long, difficult, yet exciting road, filled with many challenges. I had fun during those two years and created friendships that have lasted for over thirty years—but those years were also two of my most difficult years. I remember one day when I was overcome with the jitters of having to present a class paper. I rushed to get to class on time, only to trip going up the marble stairs to the classroom. I fell backwards and landed on the bottom of the staircase. I couldn't move, and finally someone found me sprawled out on the bottom of the stairs. I had dislocated my shoulder and had to be taken to the hospital. I spent the day in the emergency room, sedated while two nurses and a doctor pulled the shoulder back into place. Of course I missed my presentation, and when I was finally able to get back to class two days later, I was wrapped up in a shoulder cast for a few weeks and had friends take class notes for me. But that was nothing—I already had ground my teeth (from nerves) so badly that I had inflamed all of the muscles in my sinuses and the optic nerve. This caused double vision, which could only be corrected after three months of wearing a patch over one eye. In order to stop the grinding, I also had to wear a retainer in my mouth for the same period of time. So there I was, going to class with my arm in a sling, a patch over one eye, and a retainer in my mouth. I was, literally, a mess. Talk about obstacles! I then had to take leave from the program for a week and travel home for extensive medical tests, since the doctor told me of the possibility of a brain tumor. It turned out to be optic nerve inflammation, and I finally improved with the help, again, of some wonderful friends and professors. On the day of my oral comprehensives, I donned a brand-new pink suit, which I had bought specifically for the occasion. I was the first of my classmates to enter the exam room and face three of my professors for the final oral comprehensives. After the exam, I was also the first in my class to announce, along with my professors, that I was now going to carry the diploma of a JCL degree. My classmates, who were waiting outside the classroom to hear the good news, applauded, hugged, and high-fived me, then popped open a bottle of the best champagne (it was 10:00 a.m., but no one cared). They were there to congratulate me on my success—despite the obstacles.

    There were plenty of obstacles set in my path during those two years—and it all turned all right in the end. Thank God for the kindness of friends—my classmates and my professors, who helped me during the most difficult times. I seemed to have forgotten that I did not have to face all the obstacles by myself—God sent me kindness through Margaret and Michael, Cathy, Bob, Meg, Dr. Green, Dr. Kennedy, Dr. Orsy, and other wonderful classmates and professors. And one lesson I learned was to never forget that God was there, through it all, along with the kindness of friends. Thank you, CUA and JCL graduating class of 1989.

CONSIDER THE FOLLOWING

- Name occasions in your life that appeared to be filled with obstacles. Did you meet kindness on the way of surmounting those obstacles? Explain.

- What do you think of the phrase "God never gives us anything that God does not also give us the strength to handle"?

- When you have faced very difficult obstacles in your life, who was there to offer you the kindness you needed at that time?

17

Prayer: A Rather Intense, and "In Tents," Experience

"In the same way, the Spirit helps us in our weakness. We do not know what we ought to pray for, but the Spirit himself intercedes for us through wordless groans."
—Romans 8:26 NIV

"When you pray, do not keep on babbling like pagans, for they think they will be heard because of their many words. Do not be like them, for your Father knows what you need before you ask him."
—Matthew 6:7 NIV

"Rejoice always; pray without ceasing; in everything give thanks; for this is God's will for you in Christ Jesus."
—1 Thessalonians 5:16-18 NASB

"Keep watching and praying that you may not enter into temptation; the spirit is willing, but the flesh is weak."
—Matthew 26:41 NASB

In a religious community, preparation for final profession is a rather important and serious undertaking. When one commits to marriage, the vows one makes are forever, and it is the same with religious vows. All three vows of poverty, chastity, and obedience define one's relationship to God. The religious sister gives her life in love and service within a specific religious community with its individual charism and gifts. That life is given in service to God. This gift of one's life is given forever.

I very clearly remember the day that I walked through the convent doors for the first time. It was September 8, 1965. I shed my "civilian" clothes in exchange for a black dress, black stockings, and black oxford shoes. There were fifteen of us doing the same thing that day. It was called "Entrance Day." Once we changed into this simple dress, we were able to go out the doors one last time to say good-bye to our family, and then we went back through the convent doors, which then closed behind us. We said good-bye to our families, our pasts, and even our names, which we also left in exchange for a new one. It was a shocking and traumatic experience.

For the next nine years, we discerned and prepared for the day when we would actually say "forever" to this way of life. Up until that time, we had been making yearly promises, but not final vows. The day would come when we had to make a decision as to whether we were ready to take that step. There was a popular book out that summer—it was called *Should Anyone Say Forever?*[xxii] Every chance we had, we would run to the resource library and read a section of the book to find out the answer. Should anyone really say forever to anything? All things in life seemed uncertain; certainly "forever" seemed like such an unknown territory to all of us.

In preparation for this moment, our formation director had an idea—and that alone always made us nervous. That idea was set in motion when all nine of us

Prayer: A Rather Intense, and "In Tents," Experience

set off for a trip to Mount Savior Monastery, which is a Benedictine monastery located near Elmira, New York. There we gathered the summer before final vows to see if we were really up to the commitment. In preparation, we were to enter into an experience of solitude on the mountain. After all, Jesus went up the mountain to pray before making a serious decision, and that was what we were going to do as well. So we gathered at our little house, which we rented from the monks, and we were told to pick a mountain, take our gear, and set up a tent on the mountain. Now, I don't mean this figuratively, I mean this literally—we were actually told to pick a mountain (we were surrounded by them), take our gear (the equipment needed to set up a tent), and spend the next fourteen days in solitude, contemplating the meaning of the word "forever." So off we went on a pilgrimage from mountain to mountain, helping each one set up her tent, praying with her, then moving on, until we each were alone on our own mountain with the stars as our only companion, along with the strange creatures of the night, and as Simon and Garfunkel often reminded us, alone with the "sound of silence" as our guide.

There is a lot to be said about those next fourteen days—we had our manual labor each day, and prayer with the monks—but the rest of the day was spent at our tent, alone, asking ourselves and our God if we were ready to say forever.

Oh, there is so much to say about the experience. Some funny things happened that week, like wild dogs sniffing my tent; I stopped breathing for quite a while. Then Sister John the Baptist attacked a snake in the middle of the night and I'll tell you, that sucker (the snake, that is) didn't have a chance. But, if I learned anything those next fourteen days, I learned how to pray. Some of my prayers were pretty pathetic and selfish, for example:

O my God, I am heartily sorry.
O my God, I am hardly sorry.
O my God, what am I doing here?
O my God, please help me.
O my God, who ate my shoes?
O my God, what is that noise?
O my God, please don't let it rain.
O my God, I'm afraid of thunder.

In case you're interested, we all survived, and we all made it to final vows—but only by the grace of God. That summer I learned how to pray. Certainly I had prayed before then, of course. As a child I learned how to pray. My mom taught me the rosary, and when days were tough, we would pray with her as we knelt together, pleading to the Blessed Mother for enough money to pay the bills, for our neighbor's dog Lucky who disappeared, and for the violence on our street to end. I learned all of the decades of the rosary from Mom. And from Dad I learned that "singing is praying twice" as he and my sister and I would rehearse the hymns we would be singing in the church choir for the following Sunday. Then, of course, the nuns taught me how to pray—we recited our prayers every day in school, and we learned the importance of memorizing prayers so that, when times were tough, the words would just flow from our lips as a rhythm of tenderness into the heart of God. These early rituals became a part of my life and formed within me a certainty that God cared about me, and that my prayers could reach God wherever God may be.

Of course, entering the convent was like entering a school devoted to the art of learning to pray. Certainly we all know that prayer is truly an art, which only comes with practice and experience. This I learned in the convent, and in the chapters of my own life.

Yes, I learned to pray from my parents, from the nuns who taught me, and from my earlier days in the convent, and I learned how to pray in a tent on a mountain quite some time ago. I learned, and I continue to learn today, that God does not need to be told anything about what I need and want. My words in prayer are not for God's instruction but my own. I learned, from reading the writings of holy men and women, that there is no right or wrong way to pray—that we can each find our own way and that God does the rest.

If the world needs anything today, it certainly is prayer. Maybe it's time for all of us to go up the mountain and pray—pray that in our place of work, and in our place of worship, we may come to understand that we are all under the same God. We can pray that transformation can take place and that prayer can make a difference in a world that needs it, and that our prayer will rise like incense, the raising of our hands like an evening oblation.

CONSIDER THE FOLLOWING

- How do you pray? Do you have a special place of prayer?

- Who taught you to pray? Do you have a special prayer ritual (place, time, special daily prayer)?

- How do prayer and kindness relate?

18

Memory-Keepers

"Your word I have treasured in my heart."
—Psalm 119:11 NASB

"I will ask the Father, and He will give you another Helper, that He may be with you forever."
—John 14:16 NASB

"For God so loved the world, that He gave His only begotten Son, that whoever believes in Him shall not perish, but have eternal life."
—John 3:16 NASB

"Do you not know that your body is a temple of the Holy Spirit who is in you, whom you have from God, and that you are not your own?"
—1 Corinthians 6:19 NASB

"Jesus said to him, "I am the way, and the truth, and the life; no one comes to the Father but through Me."
—John 14:6 NASB

If you were baptized Catholic as a child and if you attended Catholic grammar school, then you certainly remember the Baltimore Catechism. This was your religious education training. You learned, at an early age, that God made you, and God loved you, but you had to do all you could to remain on God's "good side." Then, if you were prepared to endure the rigors of Sister Mary Liquori's Monday morning class recitation of the Ten Commandments, the spiritual and corporal works of mercy, the mysteries of the rosary, the seven sacraments, the morning offering, and the act of contrition, you could be considered a candidate for "Soldier of Christ" for the week. You had accomplished what any soldier would be asked to do if defending their faith. You could rely on your memory to recite the fundamental, immutable, unchangeable tenets of the faith, and you could defend the church at all cost. You might even be called to be a martyr for your faith—and there could be no better glory.

Of course, we all know that being able to recite the answer to catechism questions is not what makes one a good Catholic. Being a good Catholic, and defending your faith, is so much more than memorizing standard answers from a catechism book.

At the same time, I can't help but wonder if the pendulum has swung too far in the opposite direction. Have we decided that any form of memorization with regard to our prayers or other facts of our faith is simply an outdated and old-fashioned way of teaching religion?

In "Learning by Heart," a chapter in the National Directory for Catechesis (2005), the US bishops proposed the memorization of "the principal formulations of the faith, basic prayers, key biblical themes, personalities and expressions and factual information regarding worship and Christian life."[xxiii] The function of such knowledge, they say, is not to promote "rote religion" on the model of the Baltimore Catechism. Rather, the purpose is to "strengthen Christian identity and unity, providing an accurate exposition of the faith for the developing of

Christians and a common language which is to express, share and celebrate."[xxiv]

Memorization can be good for the soul—it can strengthen our mind as well as nurture our faith. I remember three distinct moments in my life when memorized prayer helped me through despair. I remember, in these moments, that I wanted so desperately to be connected with God; I wanted to pray, yet I could not find words. It was at those moments that I found my mouth moving in words that drew up from my breath just as simply as the breath itself.

The words spoke of a "Father who art in heaven" (Matthew 6:9 ASV).

The words spoke of a Lord who "is my shepherd; I shall not want" (Psalm 23 KJV).

The words spoke of a Father into whose "hands I commend my spirit" (Luke 23:46 KJV).

The words spoke of a Lord who "is my light and my salvation; whom shall I fear?" (Psalm 27:1 KJV).

The words asked, "My God, my God, why have you forsaken me?" (Matthew 27:46 NIV).

The words from long-forgotten prayers, the words from the Scriptures, became my words when I had no words—they became my prayer when I could not find my own. The words became an expression of my belief when I felt helpless to believe at all. Moments of helplessness, grief, and illness were moments when the words from familiar psalms, from Scripture, and from lost but memorized prayers, surfaced from my memory and made a home in my heart, and I felt saved. What was I saved from? I'm not sure; maybe saved from despair, saved from a feeling of emptiness, perhaps, but saved, nonetheless, by the grace of God.

All of us are teachers, in one form or another. However, if we have children, or are teaching children, it is even more of a challenge than ever before to instill in them the importance of knowing and understanding their faith. Memorization can be one tool—not the only tool—

but one in which we and they can connect with Catholics throughout the world in a common language. It might be better that they recite their prayers, rather than the words to some music videos. Kindness can come from what we recite—if the words of such prayers can be spoken in our hearts, to words on our tongues, then those same words can be turned into actions that can make a difference in our world.

So—let's work together to revive and restore our common language, the language of our faith, knowing that the words that are spoken by the heart are, and can also become, the words from our heart—and perhaps, from the depth of our heart. Amen.

CONSIDER THE FOLLOWING

- What does it mean to say that "kindness can come from what we recite—if the words of such prayers can be spoken in our hearts, to words on our tongues, then those same words can be turned into actions that can make a difference in our world?"

- How can memorized prayer help in times of crisis?

- What does it mean to "pray without ceasing"?

19

Where Have All the Manners Gone?

"And as you wish that others would do to you, do so to them."
—Luke 6:31 ESV

"Finally, all of you have unity of mind, sympathy, brotherly love, a tender heart, and a humble mind."
—1 Peter 3:8 ESV

"Do nothing from rivalry or conceit, but in humility count others more significant than yourselves."
—Philippians 2:3 ESV

"Let no corrupting talk come out of your mouths, but only such as is good for building up, as fits the occasion, that it may give grace to those who hear."
—Ephesians 4:29 ESV

> "Do you not know that your body is a temple of the Holy Spirit within you, whom you have from God? You are not your own, for you were bought with a price. So glorify God in your body."
> —1 Corinthians 6:19-20 ESV

> "It is not what goes into the mouth that defiles a person, but what comes out of the mouth; this defiles a person."
> —Matthew 15:11 ESV

The other day a friend told me a joke. It goes like this: What do you call an alligator who wears a vest? Answer: An investigator. Okay, so you laughed—good. It may be a little corny, but at least amusing. This topic is not really amusing, however, nor is it about alligators, but it was my friend's search for alligator jokes on the internet that brought me to this topic. When she did a web search on alligators, she happened upon a website from Disney that was entitled "Can you teach my alligator manners?" Unless I meet a lot of alligators during the day, I suspect that I won't need to worry about it, but I did wonder how we can teach manners to people—many people we meet, or just see in public, or perhaps even work with, appear to have lost a sense of politeness, respect, and just plain good manners.

Lynn Truss writes, in her book *Talk to the Hand: The Utter Bloody Rudeness of the World Today*, that nothing could be simpler than to learn the words "thank you" and "please." She states: "The reason I have begun with "please" and "thank you" is that nothing could be simpler than to learn these words. That's what we say to ourselves every day. They are only words! They cost nothing! Also, they are in limitless supply and are miraculously immune to the dangers of over-use."[xxv]

Where have all the manners gone? There are times when I find myself pretty fed up with the lack of manners in our society today.

First point: Where have all the manners gone when it comes to speech? What has happened to our speech? Why do some people have the need to swear in order to get their point across? Swear words come from people's mouths, from their e-mails, texts, and Facebook pages. I'm sorry—I simply don't get it. I tried it once (swearing, that is) to see if it made me feel better, thinking maybe that's why people swear. So, I tried it while in the shower the other day, pretending that I was one of those old-time cussing cowgirls. It didn't work. Actually I felt sick to my stomach and figured I must be an old prude. Perhaps I am an old prude, but I prefer to be a prude and proud of it, rather than one who has to depend on swear words to get her point across.

Second point: Where have all the manners gone when it comes to human respect? I gave a workshop once to a mostly friendly and dedicated group of people. I had never met most of these people before and was rather looking forward to the gathering and the exchange of ideas. But what right does someone have to criticize and berate the presenter in public? I can understand and respect constructive criticism—I appreciate it, especially when it presents an opposing opinion leading to an open discussion or another point of view. However, this did not appear to me to be the case. This person's treatment of me came from anger—for whatever reason, it was uncalled-for and downright rude. What made this even worse, however, was that while I was trying to answer this person's illogical objections to what I was saying, a crying baby was right in front of me. It didn't seem to bother the parents that the baby was yelling right in my ear. I don't think the baby followed my presentation real well, nor do I think she belonged right in the front row, possibly drooling down the front of my newly pressed skirt.

Which leads me to my third point of, where have all the manners gone when it comes to the amount of bullies walking around, and why do we give them power? Why do some people have to yell to get their point across, or play the bully game and act like they are better than everyone else? What happened to respecting authority or personhood? Is that gone as well?

Some examples of bad manners were revealed by some people I interviewed—this is what they reported as bothering them the most when it comes to bad manners.

People showing up late for work or for meetings.

Certainly, good manners tell us that if we are going to be late for meetings, or for work, then we let our supervisors know. But how about our supervisors? Do they let their employees know if they will be late? Because, let me tell you, a department looks pretty bad if visitors or customers call looking for the supervisor, and we haven't a clue as to where our supervisor is, or, whether he/she will be in late, or whether he/she will be coming in at all.

People answering a cell phone or texting during a meeting.

Many people I spoke with claim that they find this very rude, but at the same time, they admit that they themselves are guilty of it. I would take this even further—I have gone out to dinner and seen two or three people sitting at a table, none of them speaking to each other. Why? Because they were all texting, reading their e-mails, taking a picture of their food for their Facebook page, etc. I am not talking about momentary texting or e-mailing. I'm talking about a good part of the meal. Maybe it's none of my business, but I thought dining out was a special time to share with the people you are dining with. So, I'm announcing it now: please don't show up at my table if you are too busy to look at me, talk to me, or listen to me. And don't invite me to dine with you again, because I will have more important things to do—like sorting out my sock drawer.

People claiming that pressure at work is the main cause of their bad manners.

Give me a break!! There is no excuse for bad manners—no excuse for a lack of kindness and respect.

What can we do to restore the name of good manners? Perhaps we can challenge one another to change our ways, and be more aware of our actions and behavior. It's pretty simple. It feels good to do good, and sometimes the simplest gesture of kindness can change your day.

CONSIDER THE FOLLOWING

- What simple gesture can we do to encourage better manners in our world today?

- In what areas would you like to see improvement when it comes to manners?

- How can the simplest gesture of kindness change your day?

20

Better to Give a Blessing Rather Than the Finger

"We are fools for Christ's sake, but you are prudent in Christ; we are weak, but you are strong; you are distinguished, but we are without honor."
—1 Corinthians 4:10 NASB

"But God has chosen the foolish things of the world to shame the wise, and God has chosen the weak things of the world to shame the things which are strong, and the base things of the world and the despised God has chosen, the things that are not, so that He may nullify the things that are, so that no man may boast before God."
—1 Corinthians 1:27-29 NASB

Have you ever been called stupid or fat, lazy or useless, or worse, a fool? There are a lot of hurtful words in our vocabulary, and when these words are unleashed at us like a dagger they can do irreparable damage to our self-esteem.

In my work I have listened to endless stories where one spouse stays with another because their mate has convinced them that they are fat, stupid, and worthless, and therefore no one else would ever want them.

When we hear someone labeled a "fool," what image comes to mind? I daresay we don't picture someone who is intelligent, sophisticated, or prudent. Instead we might imagine someone who is stupid, without any sense or judgment. Yet there is a passage in the letter to the Corinthians where Paul calls the disciples "fools for Christ's sake" (1 Corinthians 4:10 NASB). Is he being offensive here? What is he trying to tell us? A sermon that I found online states that when St. Paul called the disciples "fools" he meant that the disciples are nothing but a "tattered bunch of captives chained together at the end of a triumphant victory procession of a conquering hero through the city, on their way to be thrown to the lions in the arena."[xxvi] He reminds them that they are "condemned... Ragged and starving losers, without a place to go except to death, without a place to stay except in the death-pen. Cursed at, they return the curse with a blessing. [...] This is nothing short of revolutionary in their experience and character. Fools as bringers of the good news of the Risen Christ."[xxvii]

Fools are people who fail to consider the consequences. "Fools rush in where angels fear to tread."[xxviii] Paul uses the Greek word for moron, dull, stupid, and silly—in the eyes of the world, an apt description of someone capable of believing that Christ is God as well as man and that he died and was resurrected into eternal life. Paul continues to paint a picture of "reckless generosity of heart, oblivious of the consequences."[xxix]

So, as Paul states, we are fools, but not just fools, he adds—"fools for Christ's sake" (1 Corinthians 4:10 NASB). What started out as pretty demoralizing and demeaning becomes the highest of compliments. We are people capable of believing that Christ died and rose again and is victorious, and when we are insulted because of our beliefs, we don't throw an insult back; instead, we give a blessing. When we are persecuted, we don't fight back; instead, we answer politely. I know a priest who was given the finger by a driver of another car when both were involved in a traffic jam. He returned this gesture with one of his own. But the gesture back to the other driver was a blessing; much like the priest would give to the congregation at the end of the liturgy. I would imagine that the person was quite surprised when she realized that she had just given the finger to a priest and a gesture of blessing was given her in return.

So—when Paul calls us fools for Christ's sake, he does not mean to degrade or malign or insult. Instead, he turns the tables on our tapestry of logical thinking. Nothing is really logical when it comes to being a follower of Christ. We might as well come to grips with that realization. Being a follower demands a change of life so radical that many may look upon us as fools. But we should not care, because the victory is ours in the end. God loves us, even if we are sometimes strangely forgetful of God... "even if our heart seems to be more attached to many things than to God, the God of our heart and our portion forever. He is the one who is faithful to us, good to us, close to us, merciful to us. He is our light."[xxx] So, for Christ's sake, if someone calls you a fool, give this person a blessing, not the finger, and politely accept the compliment.

CONSIDER THE FOLLOWING

- Name an instance in your life when you felt stupid or foolish.

- Name another instance when you were a "fool for Christ's sake."

- What does it mean to say that nothing is logical when it comes to following Christ?

21

Finding Kindness Behind the Rolling Stone (Easter)

"Early on the first day of the week, while it was still dark, Mary Magdalene went to the tomb and saw that the stone had been removed from the entrance."
—John 20:1 NIV

"The stone that was rejected by you, the builders ... has become the cornerstone."
—Acts 4:11 ESV

"As for these things that you see, the days will come when there will not be left here one stone upon another that will not be thrown down."
—Luke 21:6 ESV

"As you come to him, a living stone rejected by men but in the sight of God chosen and precious."
—1 Peter 2:4 ESV

Finding Kindness Behind the Rolling Stone (Easter)

"You are Peter, and upon this rock I will build My church."

—Matthew 16:18 NASB

"Whichever one of you has committed no sin may throw the first stone at her."

—John 8:7 GNT

Holy Week is considered one of the most sacred times of the church year. It begins with a celebration filled with palm branches and hosannas, but then continues with a complete turnaround when Jesus is condemned to death as a criminal and nailed to a cross. The story doesn't end there, either, for he rises to new life, and then our lives become changed forever. Jesus becomes revealed as God Victorious, the God of today and forever, and none of our days will ever be the same because He lives.

The Scripture readings of Holy Week present us with incredibly powerful images. We have the waving of the branches as Jesus processes down the streets of Jerusalem, being proclaimed as king. We have images of Jesus standing before Pontius Pilate and being presented with the question, "Are you the king of the Jews?" (Luke 23:3 NIV)—then what follows is his powerful response! We have the image of the women of Jerusalem, and Simon of Cyrene taking up the cross to help Jesus along the way, and the story of Veronica wiping the face of Jesus. The most powerful image of all, of course, is the image of the cross—the image of salvation. Millions of Christians gather at the cross, especially on Good Friday. They recall Jesus' passion and death and recite together, "We adore thee, O Christ and we bless thee, because by thy holy cross you have redeemed the world."

What image will you journey with this week—what image will you draw comfort from, and what image will lead you through the last days of Jesus and into his glory?

My image this week is one of the stone being rolled away. Stones are a powerful image in the Scriptures:

"The stone that was rejected by you, the builders ... has become the cornerstone" (Acts 4:11 ESV).

"As for these things that you see, the days will come when there will not be left here one stone upon another that will not be thrown down" (Luke 21:6 ESV).

"As you come to him, a living stone rejected by men but in the sight of God chosen and precious" (1 Peter 2:4 ESV).

"You are Peter, and upon this rock I will build My church" (Matthew 16:18 NASB).

"Whichever one of you has committed no sin may throw the first stone at her" (John 8:7 GNT).

The Gospel of Mark tells us that the women wanted to anoint the body of Jesus after his death; the stone in front of the tomb was going to be their obstacle to accomplishing this mission. I picture those women rushing to the tomb to anoint the body of Jesus—all the while, they are wondering who will move the stone for them. That is a big obstacle, I mean a monumental obstacle, which would take at least sixteen Roman guards to move. But this did not stop them from going to the tomb to anoint his body.

"When the Sabbath was over, Mary Magdalene, and Mary the mother of James, and Salome bought spices, so that they might go and anoint him. And very early on the first day of the week, when the sun had risen, they went to the tomb. They had been saying to one another, "Who will roll away the stone for us from the entrance to the tomb?" When they looked up, they saw that the stone, which was very large, had already been rolled back." (Mark 16:1-4 NRSV).

How did that happen? Who rolled the stone away? That was no small matter. In Jesus' day, such tombs were usually in a depression, and the stone was rolled down an incline to cover the mouth of the tomb. For a small grave, about twenty men were required to roll a stone down a hill to cover the door of the tomb. Thus, in order to roll the stone away, the women would have needed more than a full Roman guard. The stone was certainly going to be an obstacle to their getting to Jesus to anoint his body. So—what a surprise it was for them to arrive there and find that the stone had been rolled away.

In Matthew's account, there was an earthquake and an angel who descended from heaven to open the tomb. There are no such dramatics in Mark's telling, though his version is no less powerful. Mark says, "When they looked up, they saw that the stone, which was very large, had already been rolled back" (Mark 16:4 NRSV). Mark uses the Greek word *anakekulistai*, which is a perfect passive: "has been rolled away." Very often, when a verb in the passive voice is used in Scripture, it has only one meaning. God is the agent. We see this repeated in the writings of Paul and in the use of the passive verb in the Beatitudes. Pious Jews would regularly use the passive to avoid using the name of God, because God's name was too holy to say out loud. So, ultimately, Mark makes it all too clear—the stone at the door of the tomb has been rolled away because God rolled it away.

The women had to have known that they would be unable to move the stone, but they went anyway. They took it on faith that they could gain access to the tomb, even if they didn't know how. Wow—what a lesson. The women had enough faith to trust that God would take care of the obstacles. What a lesson to learn—that the stones that block our path or disrupt our vision of creating a Christian life, a Christian home, or a more

Christian workplace do not have to have the last word, because God will roll away the stone. We are not alone. Our life and our desire to perform good works do not depend solely on our ability or our strength. They depend on God and on God's grace.

So, as we find ourselves entering into the Holy Week cycle, let us greet the days with holy longing, knowing that in the end it all works out—one day everything appears hopeless, and the next day the blind can see, the lame can walk, the dead shall be raised. And when we sing our alleluias, listen very carefully ... because even the stones will shout.

CONSIDER THE FOLLOWING

- What stones have you rolled away in your life, and what did you discover beyond the rolled stone?

- What is the difference between "joy" and "Easter joy"?

- What does Easter teach us about kindness?

22

First-Class Women Are Not Second-Class Citizens

"Nevertheless, with respect to the fundamental rights of the person, every type of discrimination, whether social or cultural, whether based on sex, race, color, social condition, language, or religion, is to be overcome and eradicated as contrary to God's intent."

—*Gaudium et Spes* (Section 29)

"There is neither Jew nor Gentile, neither slave nor free, nor is there male and female, for you are all one in Christ Jesus."

—Galatians 3:28 NIV

"An important fact unknown to many within the church is that superiors of religious orders in the United States are, in many cases, battered women in the church. The form of violence is not as blatant as it is in some marriages, but the physical and mental anguish is strikingly similar. The parallels to domestic violence are unmistakable; the reasons for the silence are identical. The silence must be broken so all in the church can participate in the ministry of justice, reconciliation, and conversion."

—*National Catholic Reporter*, December 21, 1984

There are many reasons to celebrate the lives of valiant women, past and present. First of all, we have the bravery of Malala from Pakistan, who was prepared to give her life so that girls like her would have a right to an education.[xxxi] We read in the papers about women who have given their lives for their children in countries around the world, and we hear of heroic women who suffer all kinds of mental, physical, and sexual abuse in households and workplaces and through the horrors of human trafficking. It is estimated that at least 700,000 women and children are trafficked each year for sexual exploitation.

Continuing with stories of valiant women, we have two female American saints who were canonized in October of 2012 by Pope Benedict XVI—one is Blessed Kateri Tekakwitha, who grew up near Auriesville, New York,[xxxii] and the other is Mother Marianne Cope, a Franciscan Sister from Utica, New York.[xxxiii] We also have Hildegard of Bingen, who, in 2012, was given the title of Doctor of the Church.[xxxiv] Out of thirty-three named Doctors of the Church, there are only three women who have been given this honorable title. Now Hildegard sits within the ranks.

The litany of valiant women continues, and in 2013 we celebrated the fiftieth anniversary of the Second Vatican Council, a historic moment for women in the church. However, at that point in time women were only allowed at the Council as auditors (listeners), and there were fifteen of them—all brave and all valiant. I recall one story told by Sister Mary Luke Tobin—a courageous woman herself, and an auditor who was present at the Second Vatican Council. She told of how the Pastoral Constitution called "The Church in the Modern World" was being written. This was the quote that she remembers well, as it was being deliberated upon by the bishops at the commission meeting, where some of these women auditors were present: "With respect to the fundamental rights of the person, every type of discrimination, whether social or cultural, whether based on sex, race, color, social condition, language or religion, is to be overcome and eradicated as contrary to God's intent."[xxxv] Had the bishops really understood the injustices in the church's attitude toward and treatment of women, perhaps they would have paid more attention to the women auditors present as this part of the document was being written and read for review. But they didn't. When one of the authors of this document read a flowery and innocuous sentence to the commission members for their consideration, he noticed that the women auditors did not seem too impressed by what he was reading. And so, he called on Rosemary Goldie, an auditor from Australia, to comment on his statement. "Rosemary," he said, addressing the intelligent and able Rosemary Goldie, "why don't you respond happily to my praise of women and what they have contributed to the church?"[xxxvi] Pressed for a response, Rosemary answered, "You can omit all of those gratuitous flowery adjectives, along with the pedestals and the incense flowing from your sentence. All women are asking for is that they be recognized as the full human person they are, and treated accordingly."[xxxvii] Sister Mary Luke Tobin stated that she does not believe even to this day that the bishops who were present then understood what Rosemary meant to convey. This episode easily represents the state of ignorance of the problem at the time of Vatican II. During that time, many religious sisters who were working in the church knew firsthand what it meant to be treated as second-class citizens.

I think it would be difficult to find a woman today who has not experienced some form of discrimination in her home, her church, or her workplace, simply on the basis of her gender. There are times that just being a woman can feel like a "pre-existing condition."

Going down memory lane myself, I can share with you some of my repeatable stories (since many cannot be repeated). I have created my own list of "Believe It or Not":

- I remember having to sit outside a classroom to take a theology course because women were not allowed into any theology or canon law classes at that time. The professor allowed us to set up a chair outside the classroom, and he would leave the door ajar so that we could listen in on his lectures. Of course, it was different on the campus of Notre Dame University. One of our older Sisters recalled that women were also not allowed to take theology classes there—but religious nuns were, because they were not considered women.

- I remember a new assignment in a parish that was building a new parish center. I was to be their new DRE. The pastor showed me the blueprint of my new office, which gave me a spacious office with a window and a seating area. What I did not realize until later (when the pastor planned an open house to show off the new building) was that two sets of blueprints existed. One was the real blueprint, and the second set existed solely to "keep me quiet"—that's what the pastor told me later, after I realized that my office was simply a tiny cubicle at the end of the hall. He said that he didn't show me the real blueprints because he couldn't stand to "watch me fuss" about the size of my office.

- In another parish I was given a car for my ministry. One day, as I was leaving the parish at the end of a workday, I discovered that all of the hubcaps from my car were missing. I was then told that the associate pastor liked the hubcaps on my car better than the ones on his car. So he removed them and put them on his, never replacing mine. I drove for months without hubcaps on my car. Later that year, I left the parish. The parishioners had a farewell party for me in the parish hall. The associate pastor chose not to attend. It's unfortunate that he was not present, because the parishioners filled the parish hall with decorations of hubcaps.

- I remember attending many meetings where I was asked to make the coffee—but could not be a part of making the decisions. That was left to the all-male members of the organizations.

- In another parish where I worked and lived with two other Sisters, we discovered that our convent was being closed because we read about it in the church bulletin that Sunday.

Enough of that—I'm sure you get the point. If you are a woman, there is no doubt that you have experienced some form of discrimination—and, if not, your time will come, I am sure. So, as we celebrate the valiant women found in Saints Kateri and Mother Marianne, and Hildegard of Bingen, let us also celebrate all the women of the Second Vatican Council, and all the women and those great men whom we know, who daily struggle for an equal playing field for women.

Let us never forget where we've been ... and pray that we'll never be there again.

CONSIDER THE FOLLOWING

- Have you had experiences where you have been discriminated against?

- Have you had experiences where you have been guilty of discrimination?

- What positive steps can you take in order to assure your daughter and your daughter's daughter that they have a place in the church?

23

Are You Just "One of the Girls" in the Office?

"Being a girl is certainly easier than being a woman. Girls don't take responsibility for their destiny. Their choices are limited by a narrowly defined scope of expectations. And here's another reason why we continue to exhibit the behavior learned in childhood even when at some level we know they're holding us back. We can't see beyond the boundaries that have traditionally circumscribed the parameters of our influence. It's dangerous to go out of bounds. When you do, you get accused of trying to act like a man or being 'bitchy.' All in all, it's easier to behave in socially acceptable ways."
—Lois Frankel, *Nice Girls Don't Get the Corner Office*

"Asking for what you want doesn't always guarantee you'll get it, of course. As we will show, our culture often discourages women from saying what they need and responds badly when they do. "
—Linda Babcock and Sara Laschever, *Women Don't Ask*

The Side of Kindness

Everyone needs friends in their lives—those you can laugh with and cry with, those you can share intimate secrets with, and know that the secret is safe with them. For me, I call these female friends my "girlfriends"—and we celebrate once a month by having what we call our "girls night out." It is our treasured moment when we come together; we go to a show or out to dinner, and we share sacred moments of laughter and tears. These are friends that have been with me through thick and thin, good days and bad days, come rain or come shine. Yes, these are my girlfriends—I can be totally myself with them, and they with me. When I am with them, I am just one of the girls, and I use the word "girls" affectionately.

But I hear the word "girls" used at times when it's not so affectionate. For example, have you ever come across this at your workplace?

- A male employer says to another employer, "Tell the girls that the report has to be in by tomorrow."
- A female boss says to a male employer, "Tell the girls they can leave early today." Or "Go ask the girls to come into the office, please."

Now, some of these "girls" are older than their bosses, with college degrees, with children, and with years of experience in their profession. So, I am puzzled as to how and why they become girls in the office, when at home they are mothers, grandmothers, entrepreneurs, nurses, and caretakers.

- A man comes home from the store and says, "The girl behind the counter was very helpful." The girl was about forty years old. I wonder if he would have come home and said, "The boy behind the counter was very helpful."

Are You Just "One of the Girls" in the Office?

When is a female employee a "girl"—and why is she called a "girl"? Is it used as a sign of affection, a term of endearment, or is it that the "girl" is not considered an equal, but in a lower class? Could the use of that word in the workplace be more demeaning than affectionate? And, if so, where is the kindness in that?

So, perhaps we can pay more attention to the words we use when addressing one another, as well as the inflection in our voice. And if you think that when you use the word "girl" it is appropriate, try asking the "girl" what she thinks.

CONSIDER THE FOLLOWING

- Have you ever had the experience of being called "one of the girls in the office"? How did that make you feel—and did you react or respond to the person who used the phrase?

- Do you find the word "girls" an affectionate term or a demeaning term? Does it make a difference who uses it, and what the circumstances are when the word
"girls" is used?

- What other ways can we address either a male or female that can be understood as demeaning or insulting?

24

"Not Counting Women and Children"—Where's the Kindness in That?

"There is neither Jew nor Greek, there is neither slave nor free man, there is neither male nor female; for you are all one in Christ Jesus."
—Galatians 3:28-29 NASB

"In no way is God in man's image. He is neither man nor woman."
—The Catechism of the Catholic Church (370)

It's time to celebrate women—especially women in the Bible who have often been left out and ignored; those who go unnamed and unnoticed. It's time to take another look.

We know that Jesus called the twelve male apostles. But did you know that Jesus called women apostles to follow him as well? We don't read about the female apostles. That doesn't mean that there weren't any—it just means that it wasn't recorded. Where's the kindness in that?

"Not Counting Women and Children"—Where's the Kindness in That?

We know that when Jesus teaches us to pray, he starts by saying, "Our Father," but did you know that Jesus speaks about God in female terms as well? He says that God is like:

1. A woman seeking a lost coin (Luke 15:8-9)
2. A baker woman (Luke 13:21)
3. A mother hen (Luke 13:34)
4. A birthing mother and midwife (Revelation 12:2)

We know, of course, that the foundation of the church is built on Peter—that he recognized Jesus as the Son of God, and that is why he is called the head of the church. But what about Martha when she says, "Yes, Lord; I have believed that you are the Christ, the Son of God, even He who comes into the world" (John 11:27 NASB)? She also recognized Jesus as the Son of God, but we hear very little about this from the teachers of the church. Where is the kindness in that?

We know that Jacob had twelve sons, representing the twelve tribes of Israel. But did you know that he also had daughters? I bet we couldn't name them.

We know and often hear of the story of God being like the shepherd looking for the lost sheep (Luke 15:1-8). But did you know that the story of God being like a woman who found her lost coin (Luke 15:8-10) follows immediately after the passage of the lost sheep? Both stories are Jesus' way of describing God—one male image and one female image. But my guess is that children in school would recognize the story of the lost sheep almost immediately, but might not have ever heard about God being like the woman finding the lost coin. Why is that?

Did you know that Moses would have died in infancy had it not been for the bravery of women—Shiphrah and Puah (Exodus 1:15-21), Jochebed (Exodus 2:1-3), Pharoah's daughter (Exodus 2:5-10), and Miriam (Exodus 2:4-8)?

We can continue to read about the prodigal son and the other brother, and the father welcoming his son back (Luke 15:11-32). Maybe we don't bother to ask ourselves, what about his mother? Did he have any sisters, or does it even matter?

If women are not in the biblical text, it does not necessarily mean that they were not present. There is a tendency to overlook the presence of those considered less important, omitting them from the telling. For example, Mark does not mention women at the multiplication of the loaves. Matthew says, "About five thousand men had eaten. (This number does not include the women and children who had eaten.)" (Matthew 14:13-21 GWT). If Matthew didn't include the "phrase "does not include" we would be led to believe that there were no women present at all at the multiplication of the loaves. Again, where is the kindness in that?

Religious patriarchy is definitely alive and well. Many women have had first-hand experience of this very strong form of prejudice and power. If they have not, it's never too late. Consequently, the power of the ruling men is said by them to be delegated by God—invariably spoken about in male terms—and exercised by divine mandate.[xxxviii] One only has to be aware of the writings of Thomas Aquinas to understand how and to what extent this patriarchal way of thinking influenced the church. Aquinas accepted as part of the Aristotelian heritage the notion of ancient Greek biology, that the male seed carried all the potency for new life. He furthermore figured that under optimum conditions, men, who are the pinnacle of creation, would reproduce their own perfection and create sons. The fact is, however, that at least half of the time they generate daughters, who fall short of the perfection of the male sex. This indicates that the man was not up to par at the time of intercourse. Perhaps his seed was damaged, or he was "short on energy due to hot, humid weather."[xxxix] For Aquinas, the female was considered nothing short of a defective male.[xl]

In the 1983 Code of Canon Law there is an attempt to change the sexual imbalance that exists in the church. Canon 208 states, "There exists among the Christian faithful a true equality regarding dignity and action by which they all cooperate in building up the body of Christ." So there have been attempts made by some church documents to rid the law of discrimination, but it hangs there like a noose, nevertheless.

Instead, what continues to go unnamed also goes unnoticed. When women are not counted, they are then ignored, or treated as inferior to men—not only in the church, but in many businesses as well as homes today.

We need to make a resolution. Perhaps we can resolve to count women and children and to challenge one another and our church to also count them as equally effective members and leaders in the church. Together, let's resolve that we will do all we can together to live out the true message of equality and inclusiveness that has always been the message of the Gospel, but which has not always been preached as such in our churches or Catholic institutions.

Tell, me, where is the kindness in that? Let's resolve to make a change.

CONSIDER THE FOLLOWING

- Does your self-image reflect and influence your image of God?

- Do you see any irony or contradiction in the Catholic Catechism quote found at the beginning of this chapter: "In no way is God in man's image. He is neither man nor woman"?

- Choose a woman you know who continually performs acts of kindness, goodness, and faithfulness, yet goes unnamed and unnoticed today—in society and/or the church. Can you reflect on this woman as a model of faith and spirituality, and share this reflection with another?

25

Let's Move Our "But"

"For progressive Catholics, Pope John XXIII is a hero and a saint. He convoked, masterminded and led the work of the Second Vatican Council, which produced such profound reform in the life of the church. Many today look upon John as having had from the very beginning a clear idea of where he wanted the council and the church to go.

I disagree. In my judgment, John did not have a clear idea of the reform he wanted to bring about at Vatican II. In fact, I was quite disappointed with the first years of his papacy and was not expecting much to happen at the council. His greatness in my eyes is that he was open to change and growth."
 —Charles Curran, *National Catholic Reporter*, "Greatness in Being Open to Change: John XXIII"

Once upon a time there was a woman who prepared a special roast every Sunday night for supper. Before putting the meat in the roasting pan, she would meticulously cut off both ends of the roast, then put it in the pan, and then put it in the oven. Finally her husband asked her, "Why do you cut off both ends of the perfectly good piece of meat?" She told him that that was the way her mother always cooked it, and so that was the way she was going to cook it too. He suggested another way, and her response was, "But it's always been this way." So the next time the woman's mother came to the house, he decided to ask her why she fixed her roast that way. The mother laughed and said that when she cooked her roast, the roasting pan was so small that she had to cut both ends of the meat off so that it would fit in the pan.

This is a laughable story, but oh, so true. Sometimes we do things because that's the way it was always done—but with no logical reason behind it.

Have you ever found yourself in a situation where you make a suggestion of change, but are immediately met with the response, "But it can't be done that way because we always do it this way"? That response quickly puts an end to any conversation. When you hear that phrase, "But we always do it this way," you know that you are in for some difficulties. Introducing a new idea, a new way of operating a business, or even a new way of looking at a problem can often be a moment of insight into a new way of thinking. Yet when those moments are thwarted because of this phrase "But we always do it this way," then any possibility of change suddenly goes out the window—and you may as well go out too. (At least for the moment, that's how you feel.)

Change, for some people, is seen as such a threat that a mere suggestion of it shuts down any and all crucial conversation. This may also resonate with you when wanting to negotiate a change, a compromise, or a dialogue. If there is no room for dialogue, no room for a differing opinion, and no room for another's point of view, then there is no room for growth or change.

Consider Henry Ford and his invention of the Ford assembly line. He decided to have the cars move to the workers instead of the "but we always do it this way" of having the workers move to the cars.[xli] That simple switch revolutionized the automobile industry. How did he think of this? My guess is that he didn't know exactly what the result would be when he decided to change his assembly line. But he decided to do something that wasn't the way it had always been done.

Think about it—if you always find yourself thinking a certain way, or if you only allow yourself to think a certain way, based on previous methods, then your vision of the future will be just like your vision of the past. And those of us who are getting older have so much history that we can't imagine a new and different way of doing something. "But that's the way we've always done it."

So, when we find ourselves concentrating on the seven last words of Jesus, we can also concentrate on the seven last words that put an end to any possibility of change, or even possibility of conversion. Let's try not having our seven last words be "But we always did it this way." Instead, let's move our "but." Let's move it to the end of the sentence instead of the beginning—let's have our seven last words be "We always did it this way, but…" Let's leave room for other options, other possibilities, other ways of thinking, and other opinions, and then, let's just see what happens.

It's worth a try—and God knows, it may lead to something totally new.

CONSIDER THE FOLLOWING

- What changes have you survived in your life, which you originally thought of as negative?

- How often have you found yourself saying these words: "But we always do it this way"?

26

I May Not Be Perfect, But I Am Saved

"This above all: to thine own self be true, and it must follow, as the night the day, thou canst not then be false to any man."
—William Shakespeare, *Hamlet*

"What good will it be for a man if he gains the whole world, yet forfeits his soul?"
—Matthew 16:26 NIV

"Above all, be true to yourself, and if you cannot put your heart in it, take yourself out of it."
—Hardy D. Jackson

"Accept everything about yourself—I mean everything, You are you and that is the beginning and the end—no apologies, no regrets."
—Henry Kissinger

"Be not anxious about what you have, but about what you are."
—Pope Gregory I

I May Not Be Perfect, But I Am Saved

"Be who you are and say what you feel, because those who mind don't matter, and those who matter don't mind."

—Dr. Suess

"A bird doesn't sing because it has an answer, it sings because it has a song."

—Maya Angelou
(quoted in *Mind Your Own Bizniche!* by Mary Squire)

When I reflect back on my younger years as a Novice, I would describe myself back then as a "pleaser." I wanted to please my formation director, and I wanted to be perfect in everything I did. I wanted so badly to make a good impression—and I often thought of the passage in Scripture where Jesus is quoted as saying, "Be perfect, therefore, as your heavenly Father is perfect" (Matthew 5:48 NIV). Oh, I tried so hard. I wanted to live up to who I thought God wanted me to be. Perfection was my aim. I thought that if I were perfect, then God would love me.

Well—that was then, and this is now. I have learned a lot since my earlier and younger days. With age has come wisdom, and I have learned that God is a God who loves me no matter what I do. Perfection is not what is important. God doesn't ask me to be perfect; instead God asks me to be me—totally, completely, unashamedly me. God asks me to be my best self, and even though I am full of flaws, God accepts me.

Sometimes we find it so difficult to be "who we are called to be." We think of ourselves as so wounded that we will not recover from our own wounds of self-doubt and imperfection. We are afraid of being judged as weak or imperfect. We need to grow in self-acceptance, instead of being so concerned about what others think of us, or seeking others' approval.

We are born with only one obligation—to be completely who we are. Yet we spend so much time comparing ourselves with others, in the pursuit of excellence. We are often troubled and blocked by insecurity. Mark Nepo states that we often hide our insecurity by puffing ourselves up. "For, in our pain, it seems to make sense that if we were larger, we would be further from our pain. If we were larger, we would be harder to miss. If we were larger, we'd have a better chance of being loved. Then, not surprisingly, others need to be made smaller so we can maintain our illusion of seeming bigger than our pain." He goes on to state, however, that "history is the humbling story of our misbegotten inflations, and truth is the corrective story of how we return to exactly who we are. And compassion, sweet compassion, is the never-ending story of how we embrace each other and forgive ourselves for not accepting our beautifully particular place in the fabric of all there is."[xlii]

So, in our day-to-day living and working, let's try to take in the lessons from these great writers—let's not concentrate on comparing ourselves with someone else, or even someone else's work or worth. Let's not waste time on comparisons, or measuring up to the impossible standards that even St. John of the Cross, St. Theresa, or Mother Teresa could even reach. Instead, let us strive to be our best self—this is the real gospel message.

> When Akiba was on his deathbed, he bemoaned to his rabbi that he felt he was a failure. His rabbi moved closer and asked why, and Akiba confessed that he had not lived a life like Moses. The poor man began to cry, admitting that he feared God's judgment. At this, his rabbi leaned into his ear and whispered gently, "God will not judge Akiba for not being Moses, God will judge Akiba for not being Akiba." (From the Talmud)[xliii]

CONSIDER THE FOLLOWING

- Do you find yourself worrying a lot about what other people think of you?

- Do you find yourself seeking other people's approval for what you do or say, instead of seeking what or where your own conscience is leading you?

- What can we do to strive to be our "best self" —and what does that really mean in our day-to-day living?

- How can we work to better accept ourselves for who we are instead of trying to impress, or to become, someone else? What causes this temptation in us to always try to impress or to be someone else instead of who we really are?

27

Hope Is Only a Rooftop Away

"Everything that is done in the world is done by hope."
—Martin Luther

"We should not let our fears hold us back from pursuing our hopes."
—John Fitzgerald Kennedy

"Optimism is the faith that leads to achievement. Nothing can be done without hope and confidence."
—Helen Keller

"I know how to be brought low, and I know how to abound. In any and every circumstance, I have learned the secret of facing plenty and hunger, abundance and need. I can do all things through him who strengthens me."
—Philippians 4:12-13 ESV

"Be strong, and let your heart take courage, all you who wait for the Lord!"
—Psalm 31:24 ESV

"Love bears all things, believes all things, hopes all things, endures all things."
—1 Corinthians 13:7 ESV

"Rejoice in hope, be patient in tribulation, be constant in prayer."
—Romans 12:12 ESV

"Be angry and do not sin; do not let the sun go down on your anger, and give no opportunity to the devil. Let the thief no longer steal, but rather let him labor, doing honest work with his own hands, so that he may have something to share with anyone in need. Let no corrupting talk come out of your mouths, but only such as is good for building up, as fits the occasion, that it may give grace to those who hear. And do not grieve the Holy Spirit of God, by whom you were sealed for the day of redemption."
—Ephesians 4:26-30 ESV

If you have ever lived in a cold—and I mean cold—climate, you may remember how long those winter months can be. Nothing but day upon day of bitter cold, day upon day of ice covering the sidewalks and streets, and the bitter numbness that seems to linger forever in one's bones as well as one's spirits. I would find myself praying each winter for release from this vast expanse of unrelenting tedium.

And, after seemingly endless months of bitter cold, I would also find myself begging God to send me a sign that this would soon pass and sun and spring would again visit the earth and the soul would again sing of life and hope. And just when all seemed to be lost, suddenly, without warning, God would send me a sign—and that sign was the cooing of the mourning dove upon the roof across the street. This sound had been absent all winter and every winter. But when the snow began to melt, and the sun began to rise a little earlier, and the buds began to peek out from under the wet blanket of snow, then the cooing sound of the mourning dove could be heard—and life was filled with hope once again. Spring was on its way.

This pattern would repeat itself every year. Just when I was ready to give up and accept the fact that survival was all there was—then, suddenly, out of nowhere, except from the roof across the street, was the sound of the mourning dove, and again I was saved from despair. The mourning dove was there to tell me not to give up. And so the dove became a symbol for me, not only of the end of winter and the beginning of spring, but also that God was not giving up on me yet either, that hopes does spring eternal, and that after a long period of waiting, God still waits for me.

Symbols can be powerful. Mark Nepo speaks about the power of symbol in his book *The Book of Awakening*. He states that people throughout the ages have always saved scraps of their experience to help remind them of a memory or experience that can't be seen, but can be brought to life by symbol:

> "Someone picks up a shell at the ocean to remind them of its depth and beauty. A song sung by a choir, heard on the car radio, or walking through a mall can suddenly transform one's thoughts to another time and place. Someone saves a ticket stub, or a framed picture of a place that one visited or a person one loves, and instantly one is transported to another part of one's life, whether good or bad, happy or sad."[xliv]

Symbols can call into being all that lies in us and about us. They help us bear witness to the painful mystery of living. Noah had the sign of the rainbow as a promise from God, and, of course, we as Christians have the sign of the cross, which carries with it the hope of all eternity. But, we all also have signs that speak to us alone, as God's secret to us, of a time in our history that can restore us once again to life's goodness and promise of redemption.[xlv]

So, for me, the mourning dove was not just a mourning dove—it was the sign of a frozen time and place that didn't have to end in defeat, a sign that when all seems to be despairing, hope still exists and God has not given up on me yet.

So you can imagine my surprise when one day last week, during days when all seemed despairing and hopeless, a mourning dove decided to lay its nest in the middle of my petunia plant, which rested on the railing of my porch. I woke up one morning to the cooing sound of the dove, and watched as day upon day the dove returned with a twig in her mouth. She was playing house, I said to myself—not realizing that she was playing house at my house, on my porch. I was honored that she felt safe enough to stay, and I found myself comfortable with this old friend who followed me from my past. Then, I began to wonder why she found me—if she had a message to send me. I remembered the message from long ago—and then, suddenly, it all began to make sense.

I had needed a sign. Life seemed a little hopeless lately—too much pressure, and tension, and questions that needed answers where there were none—none that were obvious, anyway. In the now-endless heat of the south, I felt cold and numb from wondering if all of this was really worth my while. When people you love pass on and you miss them so, and when people you thought you knew turn out to be strangers, and when the work of your Sisters becomes discredited because of some focus on rules, it leads you to wonder and question if this was all worth it in the end. I needed a sign, and God knew that, and sent me one. God says don't despair—don't give up—I send you the dove.

What is your symbol? What is God sending you? When you are ready to hang it up, or give it up, or when you feel that your work has no meaning or its meaning has been stolen from you, then it may be time to discover your own symbol of hope—and once you find it, to savor its sweetness. And, if you can't find your symbol, just go outside and listen for a while—you might hear the cooing of the mourning dove from the roof across the street—and then stand there in awe at the mystery of God's incredible promise.

P.S. When reading about the mourning dove, I discovered that Mom and Dad mate for life, and both take care of the nesting of their new brood of baby doves. After they are born, the mom stays with the babies during the day and is replaced by Dad for the night shift. I watched the "changing of the guard" each day as one replaced the other. Here I was, thinking that Mom had been abandoned by Dad when it was time for the real work to begin. I was wrong. He was there for the night shift. Mom and Dad together, male and female together, share the load together, and share the responsibility. Another sign in this world of contrast and opposites, showing us that there is still hope that we can work together as one.

CONSIDER THE FOLLOWING

- When you feel that you are losing hope, who or what do you turn to for courage or renewed vision?

- Do you have a hero in your life who gives you hope and becomes a model of courage for you?

- What gifts do you have that you can pass on to others to help them in times of despair?

28

Because Others Are Mean Is No Reason Why I Should Be

"Put away from you all bitterness and wrath and anger and wrangling and slander, together with all malice, and be kind to one another, tenderhearted, forgiving one another, as God in Christ has forgiven you."
—Ephesians 4:31-32 NRSV

"Because they are mean is no reason why I should be. I hate such things, and though I think I've a right to be hurt, I don't intend to show it."
—Louisa May Alcott, *Little Women*

"Everything is funny, as long as it's happening to somebody else."
—Will Rogers

"It gets so tiring, this strong-picking-on-the-weak stuff. It was the story of my life – literally – and it seemed to be a big part of the outside world too. I was sick of it, sick of guys like these, stupid and bullying."
—James Patterson, *Maximum Ride: The Angel Experiment*

"I have a deep-down belief that there are folks in the world who are good through and through, and others who came in mean and will go out mean. It's like coffee. Once it's roasted, it all looks brown. Until you pour hot water on it and see what comes out. Folks get into hot water, you see what comes out."
—Nancy Turner, *Sarah's Quilt*

"Seems to me that people are mean or evil because they are scared, mostly, or in pain, or afraid they're going to lose something."
—Barbara Samuel, *The Sleeping Night*

It was a long, long time ago (I will leave you guessing as to how long) when I was a cheerleader for my high school basketball team. It was great fun to energize the fans and encourage team spirit. I was in a newly built Catholic high school, and it took many years after I left that high school before the team showed any kind of potential. But we were solid and loyal, and we cheered our team until we were blue in the face. And, when we lost, we came back the following week all enthusiastic again and ready to play. Winning wasn't everything and losing wasn't the end of the world.

But today, things have changed in our society. I don't mean to say that there weren't some levels of inappropriate behavior in the fans and in the stands when I was growing up. But it seems nothing compared to what is happening today.

Take for example what happened in sports games recently:

First, there was a wild card playoff for the World Series, the Braves vs. Cardinals—because of the controversial infield fly rule, the Braves fans became upset and began throwing things out on the field. This behavior caused at least a twenty-five-minute delay in the game while officials tried to clear up the debris and make sure that no official or player was hurt by the hurled bottles, cans, and other garbage. Fans resorted not only to name-calling, but also to violence in order to express their displeasure at the call.[xlvi]

Next, there was the NFL—the crowd at Arrowhead Stadium booed Kansas City Chiefs quarterback Matt Cassel throughout a Ravens 9-6 win at an NFL game, and someone paid for an airplane to fly above the stadium before the game with a banner that called for Cassel to be benched. Then, some Chiefs fans cheered after Ravens defensive tackle knocked Cassel out of the game with a hard hit in the fourth quarter.[xlvii] Nothing like cheering when someone gets injured...

Then there was the Georgia and South Carolina college football game. When the Georgia linebacker Christian Robinson returned from the Bulldogs' lopsided loss at South Carolina, he found his house that he shared with quarterback Aaron Murray "egged and rolled." He later posted on Twitter, "It seems that people turn on you when you are not perfect."[xlviii]

These are just some examples—oh, sure, the Braves incident as well as a house being egged is only minor, right? It's nothing like the young man in California who can no longer care for himself because he was attacked outside of Dodger Stadium for being a San Francisco Giants fan. He was beaten into submission. He finally came out of a coma and now lives in a wheelchair.[xlix]

Of course, sports fans do not have a monopoly on this kind of behavior. All we have to do is look at the political arena to experience the gladiator-like scene every day on cable news shows, in blogs, and at rallies. Divisive and mean-spirited debate within political circles is encouraged. Members who far exceed the bounds of normal and respectful discourse are not viewed with shame but are treated as celebrities, rewarded with cable television appearances, and enlisted as magnets for campaign fundraisers. It has become almost impossible to sit down and discuss a differing political view with someone without a fierce battle turning ugly. Talk show hosts do not help to create civil debate and neither do the political ads and campaign slogans.

What has happened to civil disagreement? Is it not possible anymore to hold a differing opinion than your friend, coworker, family member, or opposing team, and express it without fear of being intimidated, mocked, or treated like the enemy who must be annihilated in some way or fashion?

So, I need to give a big hurray to the Knights of Columbus, who have launched a national, nonpartisan initiative to give voice to Americans' desire for civility in public discourse.[l] They recognize that too often we have reflected the political divisions of our culture rather than the unity we have in the body of Christ. They came together to urge those who claim the name of Christ to "put away from you all bitterness and wrath and anger and wrangling and slander, together with all malice, and be kind to one another, tenderhearted, forgiving one another, as God in Christ has forgiven you" (Ephesians 4:31-32 NRSV).

I also found what is called the "Better Angels Statement," written in August of 2012 as an attempt by religious leaders across the country to call for a more civil tone before our country is torn apart. Perhaps their message can help us to get through some of the meanness in our society with some dignity left. Let's see if we can help each other as leaders in our work, our churches, and our neighborhood. "As people of faith, let us lead by example, modeling civil discourse with and respect for those with whom we disagree."[li]

Perhaps, as an act of kindness, let us lead by example—whether it is in the sports arena or the political arena, or in the actions of our everyday life. This is the least we can do.

Because Others Are Mean Is No Reason Why I Should Be

CONSIDER THE FOLLOWING

- Do you agree with Barbara Samuel's explanation that people are mean because they are scared? Explain. If you don't agree, why do you think people are mean?

- What positive steps can you take to bring kindness back?

- Can you take the "Better Angels Statement" and resolve to put it into practice in your own life?

29

Don't Just Do Something, Stand There

"Be still, and know that I am God; I will be exalted among the nations, I will be exalted in the earth."
—Psalm 46:10 NIV

"Rest in the LORD and wait patiently for Him."
—Psalm 37:7 NASB

"The LORD will fight for you; you need only to be still."
—Exodus 14:14 NIV

"Teach me, and I will be quiet; show me where I have been wrong."
—Job 6:24 NIV

"We are to seek God in all situations. The busyness that is so much a part of our lives can take its toll on us if we do not learn how to balance work, prayer, and leisure. The practice of pausing throughout the day in order to get in touch with the soul has deep roots in monastic life.

It is not easy to step aside from our work, take a cleansing breath, and ask ourselves soul questions."
—Macrina Weiderkehr, *Seven Sacred Pauses*

Last week I went with some friends up to the Smoky Mountains to make a retreat. The setting and scenery around the retreat center were so beautiful that they appeared to form a halo of glory in the sky. You would think that, being immersed in such beauty and peace, it would be easy to enter into the spirit of the retreat. However, I soon realized that I needed to learn how to be still before I would be able to really understand and hear the message from God.

Fortunately for me, the theme of the first day of retreat was "Be still." I had forgotten how to do that. Perhaps you can relate to this from your own life experience. When you are surrounded by the chaos of tasks and obligations from home and work, do you find it difficult to stop the chaos that is also running around in your head? To learn how to be still is such an important lesson for all of us, and I soon realized that I was out of practice.

However, on the third day, while I was sitting still and gazing at the beautiful view outside my window, a story I once read popped into my head from nowhere. I went in search of the book where I first read this story, and I knew without a doubt that its message was for me:

> "An old rabbi crossed the village square each morning on his way to the temple to pray. One morning a guard accosted him saying, "Hey, Rabbi, where are you going?"
> And the old rabbi said, "I don't know."
> The guard was furious. "Don't get smart with me," he bellowed. "Every morning for twenty-five years you have crossed this square to go to the temple to

pray. You know very well where you're going."

Then the guard grabbed the old man by his coat and dragged him off to jail. Just as he was about to throw him into a cell, the rabbi turned to him saying, "See what I mean, I don't know." (Joseph Goldstein)[lii]

That story may have many a lesson, but for me, it had one that I needed to hear. We don't really know what today will bring, and today may be all we have. An unexpected suffering or sorrow can force its way through the door of our lives, unannounced, and suddenly everything is changed. Loved ones who are with us one day can be snatched from us without warning; a sickness can enter our bodies and take over our energy and our spirit. When I finally took the time to be still, to pause, to stop the busyness in my head, and to listen to where God was directing me, it was only then that I could hear God's message. I realized that I only have today. I only have the precious moment of the present. Beyond that we don't really know. All of a sudden, what just a few days ago seemed so important now no longer was, and what took up my time and weighed me down no longer seemed like a heavy burden after all. It was the "being still" and the "sacred pauses" that I had during these quiet days that helped me to hear the message of "today." "As has just been said: 'Today, if you hear his voice, do not harden your hearts'" (Hebrews 3:15 NIV).

I promised myself that I would make no resolution on this retreat—since I never am very good at keeping them—but I did make a promise to myself, and that is to see each day as a gift from God. I beg you to do the same. There are not many moments to be still while we're at work, but perhaps once in a while, as you go from desk to desk, office to car, or copy machine to conference room, you might consider a sacred pause, a single moment when you can stop and remind yourself of who you are and where you are and why you are—and perhaps, it is in that single moment that God might send you a message that you need to hear and that can change your life. And since we do not know what we will face tomorrow, whether well or ill, perhaps it will be good to listen to what God has to say to us today. Perhaps this sacred pause, or moment of stillness, can help us to enter into harmony with ourselves, with our God, and with our world. If we do this, can you imagine what kind of world this would be?

CONSIDER THE FOLLOWING

- What can you do differently in order to see each day as a gift from God?

- How would you live differently if you knew you only had one more day to live?

- How can you practice being still? Would anything change in your life if you learned how to make that a daily practice?

30

Hurray for Vatican Council II

"Come, let us worship and bow down,
Let us kneel before the LORD our Maker.
For He is our God,
And we are the people of His pasture and the sheep of His hand."

—Psalm 95:6-7 NASB

"Which in time past were not a people, but are now the people of God: which had not obtained mercy, but now have obtained mercy."

—1 Peter 2:10 KJV

I can't think of anything that caused more uproar in religious circles than the slow disappearance of the religious habit. Religious sisters used to be well recognized wherever they went because of the unique habit they wore. There was the veil, the bandeau (the white head binding), the wimple (front and shoulder covering), and the scapular (the floor-length folded skirt). The habit itself was identified with the very image of the sisterhood.

Then came Vatican Council II, and everything changed. Some habits seemed to disappear overnight. Some changed gradually. But the question arose as to whether the sisterhood itself would disappear along with the habit. Religious communities adapted to the changes of the habit, some slower or faster than others—but change certainly occurred. With the publication of the documents of Vatican II in 1965, the Pope encouraged religious communities to modify their dress code to adapt more to the needs and the signs of the time. This was the "habit revolution." This was a time that I remember so well.

To the outside world, the most significant change in religious orders was the change of the habit. However, to those within the walls of the convent, the greatest changes that took place were in the living and practice of religious life itself. These changes took place because of Vatican Council II. It's one of those things that are difficult to explain unless you were there, unless you lived through them yourself.

Before 1965 the call to a religious vocation was considered a call to live out the "state of perfection." Nuns or Sisters were to resist all forms of "worldliness" and aspire to a spiritual life that required a level of discipline more restrictive and exacting than that expected of anyone else in the Catholic religion. All the rules that governed religious life were called "The Rule." "Keep the rule," we were told, "and the rule will keep you." Contact with others was kept at a minimum, and one was often reminded of the importance of modesty—hands were to be kept folded under the scapular, and "custody of the eyes" was an unspoken rule that was understood by all.

Then there was Vatican II. I still vividly remember the day when we all lined up in the convent to receive our very own copy of the Vatican Council documents. I mean our very own copy!! We only owned two other books—one was the Bible, and the other was the

Community Book of Rules. We now had a third book that we could treasure as our very own. That same summer when the documents were promulgated, we began forming small groups for "Scripture sharing." Our relationship with God, at that point, was personal and private, but that changed with the introduction of the word "sharing." It was a whole new and personally moving experience, and it was very revolutionary to actually share your spiritual life with another person and to express it out loud in a group. That too, was because of the Vatican Council.

The Vatican Council had a profound effect on the whole church. The documents of the Council no longer defined the church as the "perfect society" but as the "People of God." The use of the vernacular, turning the altar toward the congregation, removing the altar rail separating priest and people, and inviting the full participation of the congregation in the liturgy gave a new sense of inclusion. These changes were not just novelties introduced into the liturgy, but a return to the practice of the early church. Which of course makes me wonder why, in recent years, various developments have diminished the sense of belonging at the table of the Lord, like the retranslation of the Mass into clumsy wording, or the return of Latin into our liturgy, the return of the altar railing, the return of the Mass with the priest's back to the congregation, and the restrictions on sharing the sign of peace. Sometimes it feels like the Council of Vatican II never happened, or that some perhaps like to remember it as just a big mistake. More reason, then, for us to celebrate and remember together why the Council took place—it wasn't just someone's idea of an experiment gone awry. But celebrating the events of the Council reminds us once again that the church is not the perfect society, but it is the People of God. We are the church.

As a Jesuit historian of the Council stated, the Council has moved us from "commands to invitations, from laws to ideals, from monologue to dialogue, from rule to service, from vertical to horizontal, from exclusion to inclusion, from hostility to friendship, from passive to active, from finding fault to finding appreciation."[liii] This is what we are celebrating!

Pope Benedict declared October 11, 2012 the beginning of the Year of Faith. He asked us to remember and celebrate the significant event of fifty years ago—Vatican Council II. Pope Benedict wanted us to put one year aside to study and reflect on the documents of Vatican II so that they may deepen our knowledge of the faith. More importantly, he called this a time of conversion—a call to each one of us to deepen our own faith, have confidence in the Gospel, and possess a willingness to share the Gospel. It is first and foremost, however, a personal encounter with Jesus Christ and an invitation to deepen one's relationship with Christ. Perhaps we can consider beginning every year as our own spiritual Year of Faith.

At the beginning of each year, perhaps we can remind ourselves and others to take some time to reflect personally and communally on what kind of conversion we want to enter into. Can we drape ourselves in the robe of reconciliation and kindness? Can we learn what it truly means to be kind to ourselves by a true conversion of mind, heart, conversation, inspiration, and renewal? What kind of changes are we willing to make? And what can we do together to remind all of us, as followers of Christ, that this is our church, that we are the church, and that we are called to think, speak, and act as followers of Jesus in a world that truly needs us? What can we do to help change the face of the earth?

CONSIDER THE FOLLOWING

- Have you witnessed changes in the liturgy at the church where you attend Mass? Are the changes originating from Vatican Council II or in reaction to Vatican Council II?

- Which do you experience when you experience church: the perfect society, or the people of God? Can you explain?

- What kind of changes are you willing to make in order for a true conversion of heart to take place? Relate this to kindness.

31

It's All in the Tone

"Speaking recklessly is like the thrusts of a sword, but the words of the wise bring healing."
—Proverbs 12:8 NET Bible

"Death and life are in the power of the tongue, and those who love its use will eat its fruit."
—Proverbs 18:21 NET Bible

"For we all stumble in many ways. If someone does not stumble in what he says, he is a perfect individual, able to control the entire body as well. And if we put bits into the mouths of horses to get them to obey us, then we guide their entire bodies. Look at ships too: though they are so large and driven by harsh winds, they are steered by a tiny rudder wherever the pilot's inclination directs. So too the tongue."
—James 3:2-5 NET Bible

"The young pastor's voice was tremulously sweet, rich, deep, and broken. The feeling that it so evidently manifested, rather than the direct purport of the words,

caused it to vibrate within all hearts, and brought the listeners into one accord of sympathy."
—Nathaniel Hawthorne, *The Scarlet Letter*

"Stella!!"
—Marlon Brando, *A Streetcar Named Desire*

When I was a young Sister, still in training, we all took "voice" lessons. However, the voice lessons were not for singing, but for getting our point across. I learned that the tone and volume of one's voice meant everything. We were to watch our inflection, our pauses, our volume, and especially our tone.

Sister Marie Francis would often say to us, "Angels don't raise their voices." So we had to concentrate on how we used our voices (especially in the classroom), not intimidating or frightening to little children, but stern enough in tone to provoke their attention.

Sister Marie Francis herself certainly provoked our attention. She had this habit of not finishing her sentences. For example, she would often say, while waving her finger at us, "Sisters (pause), whatever you do (pause), don't." Or, she surprised us one day when she said, "Sisters (pause), I'm expecting." It took us a while to realize that her unusual habit was that she often would not complete her sentences; she presumed that you could read her mind. For example, "Sisters, whatever you do, don't speak unless spoken to," and "Sisters, I'm expecting perfection."

However, she must have felt at times like the voice crying in the wilderness. We did not always listen to her words, but we certainly listened to the tone of her voice.

Our voice is a tool, and, used effectively, it is one of the most powerful in our toolbox. Just as important as what we say, however, is how we say it, and the tone of our voice is part of that.

If our tone conveys an undercurrent of anger or frustration, sounds distracted or preoccupied, or is heavy with sarcasm, it will influence how others hear what we are saying and how they interpret our message. A misinterpretation based on our tone will garble the message, at best, or lead to a giant misunderstanding. Misunderstanding can be the downfall of a team or of a relationship, and can create a hostile environment. On the telephone, it is even more vital to catch the tone of our voice. A listener can't see our face or watch our body language, so all they have to go on are our words and our tone. We need to make sure that the two are in harmony in order to have the most effective communication.

How can we guard against that tone? If you feel it creeping into your voice, slow down or stop, take a deep breath, and start again. Or, if you realize after the fact that your tone may have garbled your message, make amends by apologizing for sending out a mixed message, clarify it, and then move forward.

CONSIDER THE FOLLOWING

- What does it mean to have our words and our tone in harmony with each other?

- Have you had the experience where your words and your tone contradict each other? Were you misunderstood because of this?

- What does the following phrase mean to you: "Our voice is a tool, and, used effectively, it is one of the most powerful in our toolbox"?

32

Don't Worry—Be Happy

"I perceived that there is nothing better for them than to be joyful and to do good as long as they live; also that everyone should eat and drink and take pleasure in all his toil—this is God's gift to man."
—Ecclesiastes 3:12-13 ESV

"But the fruit of the Spirit is love, joy, peace, patience, kindness, goodness, faithfulness, gentleness, self-control; against such things there is no law."
—Galatians 5:22-23 ESV

"Where your pleasure is, there is your treasure: where your treasure, there your heart; where your heart, there your happiness."
—Saint Augustine

"Happiness is as a butterfly, which when pursued, is always just beyond your grasp, but which, if you will sit down quietly, may alight upon you."
—Nathaniel Hawthorne

Don't Worry—Be Happy

One of the first things we learned as novices was the importance of saying aspirations. Aspirations are those short little prayers that one can say without really thinking. Like "JMJ" (meaning "Jesus, Mary, Joseph") or "AMDG" ("Ad majorem Dei gloriam," which in English is "For the greater glory of God"). They were quick and easy to remember, and it was a way that our novice director encouraged us to follow the teachings of St. Paul to "pray without ceasing." When we would pass each other in the corridor, it was our intention to nod and whisper an aspiration. This worked most of the time. Actually, after we caught on, it worked for the first few months, until we began to circulate another aspiration that was not exactly what our novice director had in mind.

It all started when we would gather outside in the novitiate yard to learn the Constitutions, better known as our Book of Rules. This was summertime; our friends were out of school, and that meant beach weather, convertibles, boys, and Beatles music. (Remember, this was in the 1960s, and we were only seventeen or eighteen years of age.) This did not seem to mesh with long, heavy black habits, black stockings, oxford shoes, and memorizing the Constitutions. Then, when the boys would ride by with their convertibles and loud music, the temptation to give it all up was pretty unbearable. Of course, our novice director could sense this, so in her most philosophical tone of voice, waving her finger in the air as if to wave divine inspiration in front of us, she said, "You know, they're not really happy." What??? You could have fooled us—they sure looked happier than we were at that moment. They aren't happy? That got us thinking of an aspiration that we used, unfortunately, more often than JMJ or AMDG—this was "THTA" ("The he_ _ they ain't")!!

We still joke about that today; however, it takes on a new meaning, because the question constantly arises, in one's life and one's ministry: "What is happiness? What truly makes me happy?"

Is it money that brings happiness? Do you remember the Beatles song: "Can't Buy Me Love"? Maybe money can't buy love, but can it buy happiness? One article that I read stated that when people had money to spend on purchases in a certain area of their lives, then that area of life was affected by a certain level of happiness that did not exist before. For example, when people spent money on experiences related to their social life, they saw an improvement in their satisfaction with their social life. When people spent money on fitness (health clubs, fitness equipment, etc.), this increased their satisfaction in their total health. So—it appears that increases in satisfaction with a particular area of their lives also affected people's overall sense of well-being and happiness in that area of their lives. So if you spend your money on experiences, you can increase your happiness, if you spend it right.[liv]

Another article I read stated that there are different levels of happiness. One kind of happiness is a sense of calm well-being. A person sitting by a swimming pool relaxing in the sun is happy in this sense. A second kind of happiness is a feeling of pleasant excitement. A person dancing with friends at a club on a Saturday night is experiencing this kind of happiness.[lv] An interesting aspect of these kinds of happiness is that they seem to be related to people's focus on time. The calm type of happiness is most associated with a focus on the present moment. The excited type of happiness is most associated with a focus on possibilities in the future. As a result, young people are more likely to experience the excited kind of happiness than older people. Older people (who are generally less focused on the future) are more likely to experience the calm type of happiness.[lvi]

Another article focused on happiness in terms of where a person lives. A person is happiest when three basic psychological needs are satisfied where they live.

They are happy if these needs are met: autonomy, competence, and relatedness. Literally thousands of studies demonstrate the positive effect of this kind of psychological satisfaction on happiness. One study indicates that psychological needs can be met by one's community. Happy people say that they feel a sense of belonging where they live, and they look forward to coming home when they have been away.[lvii]

But what really is happiness—how do we define it and identify it? Sometimes when we meet someone we can sense almost immediately that they are not happy. They exude some kind of negative energy and one sometimes can feel exhausted in their presence. Have you ever tried to convince an unhappy person that they should be happy? It just doesn't work.

But what brings you happiness—is it being in the presence of another person, is it being in a certain place, is it material goods, or is it something deeper? Jesus describes for us what can bring happiness when he says:

> "Happy are those who mourn; God will comfort them. Happy are those who are humble; they will receive what God has promised. Happy are those whose greatest desire is to do what God requires; God will satisfy them fully. Happy are those who are merciful to others; God will be merciful to them. Happy are the pure in heart; they will see God. Happy are those who work for peace. God will call them his children. Happy are those who are persecuted because they do what God requires; the Kingdom of heaven belongs to them. Happy are you when people insult you and persecute you and tell all kinds of evil lies again you because you are my followers. Be happy and glad, for a great reward is kept

for you in heaven." (Matthew 5:4-14, GNT)

These statements are not exactly what we had in mind when looking for happiness. But true happiness does not come from outside us or from some material object. When we know we have made a difference—when life reveals a deeper meaning and we can touch and feel that deeper meaning coming from some place deep within—then we have reached happiness, not as a fleeting moment but as a lasting encounter with something beyond ourselves.

So what is keeping us from attaining true happiness? What is standing in our way? Is it lack of desire? Is it allowing the distractions of a busy life to keep us in a routine until "your life is living you" instead of the other way around? You will never feel at home until you discover, uncover, or recover your divine purpose and make it the focus of your life.[lviii]

So, perhaps we can make a resolution to be kind to ourselves this week, and the kindness is in keeping with our purpose in life: to find the true meaning of our life and live that with fullness and feeling, and never lose sight of our real purpose—and that will lead us to true happiness that no one or nothing can take away.

CONSIDER THIS FOLLOWING

- At what moments in your life do you feel truly happy?

- Which one of the beatitudes has the most meaning for you?

- How can you be kind to yourself, by being true to yourself?

33

Dress for Success

"But since we belong to the day, let us be sober, putting on faith and love as a breastplate, and the hope of salvation as a helmet."
—1 Thessalonians 5:8 NIV

"Therefore, as God's chosen people, holy and dearly loved, clothe yourselves with compassion, kindness, humility, gentleness and patience."
—Colossians 3:12 NIV

"I put on righteousness, and it clothed me; My justice was like a robe and a turban."
—Job 29:14 NASB

For some reason, the religious garb of nuns has always been a fascinating topic for discussion. Just bring up the topic and it carries with it a mix of nostalgia and strong opinions—the "way things used to be" versus the way things are today. If you think it was a fascinating topic for you, you should have been the one getting dressed every morning in this religious garb. When I entered the convent, we were very soon introduced to the traditional habit of our religious congregation. Our habit was a symbol of our consecration. But learning how to dress each day was certainly a challenge—getting every piece of clothing in the right place at the right time was another part of the challenge. Think about what made up the habit. There was the white coif, the bandeau, the white wimple. There was the tunic, the veil, the rosary, the two sets of sleeves (the larger were worn folded up or in the back to allow you to work, or folded down for ceremonial occasions or whenever entering a chapel), and don't forget the rosary, the cross, the ring, the scapular, and the oxford shoes.

When the Vatican Council published its documents in 1968, they reminded us that clothes don't make the person. The full habit at times became a distraction rather than a sign, and appropriate changes were made. Slowly, religious congregations made simple changes to their traditional habits, and they were modified to be more sensible and appropriate to time and place.

This, of course, brings me to the topic of dress. Those were the good old days, when I had no decision to make as to what I was to wear to work. I was a nun; I dressed in the habit. I owned two habits—one was for Monday through Saturday. The other habit was saved especially for Sunday attire. Now, things are different. I now decide each day what to wear and how to dress so that my appearance reflects who I am and what is important to me. In other words, I dress for success. I learned that my work is affected by my self-image. If I feel good about the way I look, this improves my ability to do a good job.

So—how do we dress? Of course, we dress differently when we are in our own environment—either at home cleaning, or relaxing, or exercising. But, how do we dress when we are in public, or at work, or representing a business or a company? I discovered that it is important to look attractive because attractiveness comes from within. If you dress well, if you pay attention to your grooming, if you cultivate that smile and come across as friendly, warm, articulate, and caring, you will also come across as attractive. Looks are all in the smile and the eyes. Smiles that light up a room are magnetic and powerful. Eyes that twinkle and are full of life are enough to make us think the whole face is good-looking. Attractiveness is also about posture and position. If you slump, you give off an aura of gloom and depression. This is unattractive and not good-looking. Your walk should be erect, proud, and assured. So should your handshake. Everything about you should be up and open, happy and confident. This is what is attractive. Your grooming should be faultless, your dress sense superb and professional. Be kind to those people who have to look at you all day—what do you want them to see?

"Dress for success" should be part of your everyday wardrobe. Every day is a day to work toward success. Your work is affected by your self-image. If you feel good about the way you look, this will certainly improve your ability to do a good job. If you look sloppy, then perhaps your work will also be sloppy. And you have heard the expression "let it all hang out." Believe you me, I would not take that literally if I were you—especially when it comes to dress. I have seen too many things hang out that should be under cover, and it does nothing for one's image or attractiveness.

There is nothing wrong with dressing for success. Be proud of how you look, think about who you represent, and dress each day as if what you do and who you are is important to you. Try it and let me know what you think!

CONSIDER THE FOLLOWING

- Do you care about your dress? Why or why not?

- What does it mean to "dress for success"?

The Side of Kindness

- What does the phrase "Clothes don't make the man" mean—or, "You can't tell a book by its cover"? How do these phrases relate to this topic?

34

Jesus Wants You to Enjoy the Danish

"Finally, brothers and sisters, whatever is true, whatever is noble, whatever is right, whatever is pure, whatever is lovely, whatever is admirable—if anything is excellent or praiseworthy—think about such things. Whatever you have learned or received or heard from me, or seen in me—put it into practice. And the God of peace will be with you."

—Philippians 4:8-9 NIV

"I will praise thee; for I am fearfully and wonderfully made: marvelous are thy works; and that my soul knoweth right well."

—Psalm 139:14 KJV

Helena was eighty-three years old, and she strode rather stoically amidst the crowd at her dinner party, welcoming all of her guests. She was dressed elegantly in her light blue summer dress, with subtle blue earrings to match. She was always stately and professional, especially during her career days. She knew the correct things to say to her clients as well as her supervisors, and she also knew how to dress and act appropriately. She never stepped out of line—she wanted to fit the profile that her boss and her career expected of her, and she succeeded. So it was noticeable to many on this particular day of her dinner party that she wore high-heeled, open-toed shoes that showed off her toenails, which were painted in sparkling purple nail polish. She so broke the rules of etiquette— and her own.

Then there was Martha. She continually proclaimed the importance of healthy eating—how many calories allowed, the amount of carbs not allowed, the red meat banished but for one day a week—and she was forever praised by her friends and coworkers for her fortitude and her commitment to losing weight and making the "healthy choice." She was good and never gave in to temptation—she was the model for everyone who had a hard time sticking to their diet. She was their star, and they all wanted to emulate her. And then I saw her, biting her nails, with a dreamy look in her eye as she stood there staring at the cinnamon blueberry Danish in the pastry shop window, guilt creeping up her spine and one phrase haunting her—"What would Jesus do?" Should she also break the rule?

Then there was Harold. He stared hard at his to-do list—the e-mails to answer, the phone calls to return, and the papers to file—then he looked up and noticed the bird singing softly on his porch, the cool breeze in the air, the clouds gliding like angels in the sky, and, for one minute, he gave up his day job. He took a rest and a deep breath, lay back in his chair, and hoped that the guilt of not doing anything for a moment would quickly fade away. He broke his own rule—and, for the first time in a long time, it felt good.

Mark Twain was quoted as saying, "Life is short, break the rules, forgive quickly, kiss slowly, love truly, laugh uncontrollably, and never regret anything that makes you smile."[lix]

And so there is laughter and purple painted toenails, a Danish too delectable to ignore, a minute hideaway from the incessant worry of work undone, the incredible need to take a break—break the rules, and laugh at it all.

How many times have we heard that "laughter is the best medicine"? Many doctors today will tell you that there are numerous health benefits to laughter. Humor can take us to "high places" where we can "view the world from a more relaxed, positive, creative, joyful, and balanced perspective."[lx] If we can view the world from this perspective it surely will have an effect on our overall health.

So—here are some activities that we can include in our everyday life. There is no harm in giving ourselves a break from the seriousness of life—and if we can laugh at ourselves and life, we can build up our immune system, which will keep us healthier and happier in the long run:[lxi]

>Watch a funny movie
>Read the comic strips in the newspaper
>Share a good joke or a funny story
>Do something silly
>Play with a pet

You can also:
>Smile
>Count your blessings
>Spend time with funny people
>Laugh at yourself

So, perhaps once in a while, let's just let it all go—give in to the smile and laugh at the world, let us laugh at ourselves and at the seriousness in which we live our lives. Or maybe the problem is that we don't live it so much as endure it and miss the fun. Let's be kind to ourselves once in a while. That kind of kindness tells us to enjoy life a little more and not take it so seriously. Let's not miss the extravagant humor of the absurdities of everyday life.

CONSIDER THE FOLLOWING

- How important is it to learn how to laugh at ourselves?

- Do you take yourself and life too seriously? How can you learn to be kind to yourself and enjoy the gifts of the everyday?

- What does this phrase from Mark Twain mean to you: "Never regret anything that makes you smile"?

35

God Is the Side of Kindness

"Pray, then, in this way: Our Father who is in heaven, hallowed be your name, your kingdom come. Your will be done, on earth as it is in heaven."
—Matthew 6:9-10 NASB

"If you then, being evil, know how to give good gifts to your children, how much more will your Father who is in heaven give what is good to those who ask Him!"
—Matthew 7:11 NASB

"God is spirit, and those who worship Him must worship in spirit and truth."
—John 4:24 NASB

"When I saw Him, I fell at His feet like a dead man. And He placed His right hand on me, saying, "Do not be afraid; I am the first and the last, and the living One; and I was dead, and behold, I am alive forevermore, and I have the keys of death and of Hades."
—Revelation 1:17-18 NASB

"The one who does not love does not know God, for God is love."

—1 John 4:8 NASB

There are certain times in everyone's life where doubt takes over—whether it is a doubt regarding a decision about a new job, or a new mate, or buying a new home, or moving to a new location, or just plain doubt about life itself. We may ask ourselves, is this really all there is—is what I have been doing really going to make a difference? Does God really care, or does God even exist? And if God does exist, why is there so much suffering in the world?

And, if we think we must be a terrible person to even think such thoughts and have such doubts, all we have to do is to read some of Mother Teresa's writings to understand that this truly holy woman had grave doubts herself, which actually haunted her for at least forty years of her life. Toward the end of her life, she even doubted God's existence, and she wrote to her spiritual director, "My own soul remains in deep darkness and desolation."[lxii] She lived without really understanding, yet her faith kept her going, since faith surpasses all understanding. She willingly sacrificed the earlier consolations she had received for the challenge of living her life in pure faith.[lxiii]

On the surface, her emptiness and lack of consolation appear shocking, but in reality she was experiencing what Catholic spirituality describes as "the dark night of the soul." There is no question that to suffer this for a forty-year period must have been a terrible trial. What it says is that this saintly nun, so dedicated to others, also bore a gigantic cross that only increased her holiness and union with God.

So—who is this God? What image do I have of God—is it God as the "just judge," the silent God who allows suffering, or is it the God who is on the side of kindness? This is the time to turn to Scripture to see what it says about who this God is. What do the Scriptures say, and what does Jesus tell us about God?

Jesus offers us a very revolutionary understanding of God compared to the Old Testament image. Jesus tells us that God is like a father, and his "Abba" image of God is the most powerful of all in the New Testament. Jesus is saying that God is like a parent—a tender and intimate parent, an Abba God. This is not an image of a vengeful, punishing God but a God who is near like a parent is to a child.

And perhaps, for the most revolutionary image we have of God, we need not look any further than Jesus himself. If we want to really understand who this God is, we look to Jesus, and it is through him that we come to see the face of God.

Jesus tells us that we see the face of God when we care for one another, in love, in generosity, in tenderness, in selflessness and self-giving. Jesus wanted people to know that if they see the face of God in loving and caring for their neighbor, then they will discover that the sacred is in their midst. We don't have to look far to find God— Jesus tells us that where there is love, there is God. God IS here—in your loving, in your caring, in your generosity, and more. God is always here—even when you are conscious of your failure, your sin, and your low status in life, and when everything seems to be going wrong. God does not leave us nor abandon us, even though we often feel this way when we are suffering.

Nowhere in Jesus' preaching or in his dealings with people is there the slightest hint of the original sin mentality that later became so pervasive in the church's worldview. The Gospel evidence of the way Jesus related with children coupled with his teaching about God surely suggests he would have been horrified by the idea of children being born into a state of utter separation from God.

Jesus' life and preaching shows us that the divine and the human are intermingled, and that to see a human person living a totally loving, gracious life is to see the face of God. We see the face of God each day in those we meet, and we offer to them our own face, in which—if it is also filled with kindness, care, love, and generosity—they will also be encountering the face of God.

There was a Sufi called Mullah Nasrudin who smuggled treasure across the border and masterfully eluded the guards. Every day for four years he would parade back and forth, and with every crossing the guards knew he was hiding expensive goods that he would sell for outrageous amounts of money on the other side. But despite their thorough searches, and despite the fact that they could see that he was prospering, they could find nothing in the saddle of the donkey he rode. Finally, years later, after Mullah Nasrudin had moved to another country, the frontier guard said, "Okay, you can tell me now. What were you smuggling?" The mullah smiled broadly and said, "My dear friend, I was smuggling donkeys."[lxiv] It makes me wonder how many times I have missed the face of God because I was too busy looking someplace else to realize that God was right in front of me.

The second reflection is from a story a friend of mine once told me. She said that God is like perfume: it is everywhere, but only once in a while, when we least expect, we get a whiff—and it takes our breath away.
Let's go on then, with faith as our guide. Yes, we can have doubts; yes, we are surrounded by sufferings on all sides. And no, I don't often understand why, but I will continue to believe that God suffers when I suffer, that God weeps when I weep, and that I don't have to look far to find God revealed in my neighbor—that God is on the side of kindness and love, and where there is love, there is God.

CONSIDER THE FOLLOWING

- What image of God from the Old or New Testament best expresses for you who God is?

- What was the image of God in your childhood? How has that changed?

- What is your image of God now? How did you arrive at this new image? (Someone special in your life, Scripture, life experiences, prayer, retreat experiences, spiritual direction, etc.)

- What face of God do you want others to see in you?

Endnotes

i   Mark Nepo, *The Book of Awakening* (San Francisco: Conari, 2011), 21.
ii Ibid.
iii Malvina Reynolds, song lyrics to "Little Boxes," accessed August 9, 2013, http://people.wku.edu/charles.smith/MALVINA/mr094.htm.
iv Mary Oliver, *Why I Wake Early,* "Why I Wake Early," (Boston: Beacon Press, 2004), 3.
v   Henri Nouwen, *Out of Solitude* (Indiana: Ave Maria, 1974), 2.
vi Jamie Stringfellow, "Just Say Yes," *Spirituality and Health,* July/August 2012, 51.
vii Ibid.
viii John O'Donohue, *Beauty: The Invisible Embrace* (New York: HarperCollins, 2004), 2.
ix Ibid., 12.
x   Ibid., 15
xi Ibid.
xii Ibid., 222.

[xiii] Phyllis McGinley, *Saint-Watching* (New York: Viking, 1969), 7.
[xiv] Ibid.
[xv] Answers.com, "Leo Tolstoy," accessed August 10, 2013, http://www.answers.com/topic/leo-tolstoy.
[xvi] The Life of Henry Ford, "Did You Know?" accessed August 10, 2013, http://www.hfmgv.org/exhibits/hf/Did_You_Know.asp.
[xvii] ThinkQuest, "Lucille Ball's Biography," accessed August 10, 2013, http://library.thinkquest.org/CR0215629/lucilleinfo.htm.
[xviii] Yahoo, "Walt Disney – an American Icon Who Lived the American Dream," accessed August 12, 2013, http://voices.yahoo.com/walt-disney american-icon-lived-american-11426476.html?cat=49.
[xix] Information on Self-Efficacy, "But They Did Not Give Up," accessed August 2, 2013, http://www.uky.edu/~eushe2/Pajares/OnFailingG.htm.
[xx] BrainyQuote, "Confucius at BrainyQuote," accessed June 12, 2013, http://www.brainyquote.com/quotes/quotes/c/confucius101164.html.
[xxi] Goodreads, "Lewis Carroll Quotes," accessed July 5, 2013, http://www.goodreads.com/author/quotes/8164.Lewis_Carroll.
[xxii] John C. Haughey, *Should Anyone Say Forever? On Making, Keeping, and Breaking Commitments* (New York: Doubleday, 1975).
[xxiii] United States Conference of Catholic Bishops, *National Directory for Catechesis*, "Learning by Heart," 2005.

xxiv United States Conference of Catholic Bishops, Pastoral Letter: *Renewing the Vision: A Framework for Catholic Youth Ministry*, 1997.
xxv Lynne Truss, *Talk to the Hand: The Utter Bloody Rudeness of the World Today* (New York: Penguin, 2005), 55.
xxvi The website of Saint Thomas Church, "Sermon for October 15, 2006," accessed August 5, 2013, http://www.saintthomaschurch.org/worship/calendar/archive/view/2046.
xxvii Ibid.
xxviii Alexander Pope, *An Essay on Criticism*, 1709.
xxix Website of Saint Thomas Church.
xxx Karl Rahner, *The Great Church Year: The Best of Karl Rahner's Homilies, Sermons, and Meditations* (New York: Crossroad Publishing Company, 1994), 252.
xxxi The website of euronews, "Pakistani schoolgirl shot by Taliban launches Malala Fund charity" accessed July 12, 2013, http://www.euronews.com/2013/04/05/pakistani-schoolgirl-shot-by-taliban-launches-malala-fund-charity/.
xxxii Katherine Long, "Those devoted to Blessed Kateri 'walking on air' about canonization," Catholic News Service, accessed July12, 2013, http://www.catholicnews.com/data/stories/cns/1200744.htm.
xxxiii Carol Glatz, "Pope advances sainthood causes of Marianne Cope, Kateri Tekakwitha," Catholic News Service, accessed August 10, 2013, http://www.catholicnews.com/data/stories/cns/1104958.htm.
xxxiv Benedictus PP. XVI, "Apostolic Letter: Proclaiming Saint Hildegard of Bingen, professed Nun of the Order of Saint Benedict, a Doctor of the Universal Church,"accessed September 15,

2013,http://www.vatican.va/holy_father/benedict_xvi/apost_letters/documents/hf_ben-xvi_apl_20121007_ildegarda-bingen_en.html.
xxxv Pope Paul VI, *Gaudium et Spes: Pastoral Constitution on the Church in the Modern World* (Vatican City, Typis Polyglottis Vaticanis, 1965).
xxxvi Mary Luke Tobin, "Women in the Church Since Vatican II," *America*, November 1, 1986, accessed August 10, 2013, http://americamagazine.org/issue/100/women-church-vatican-ii.
xxxvii Ibid.
xxxviii Elizabeth Johnson, *She Who Is: The Mystery of God in Feminist Theological Discourse* (New York: Crossroad Publishing Company, 1992), 23.
xxxix Ibid, 24.
xl Ibid.
xli About.com, "Henry Ford and the Assembly Line," accessed June 12, 2013, http://history1900s.about.com/od/1910s/a/Ford--Assembly-Line.htm.
xlii Nepo, *The Book of Awakening,* 12.
xliii Ibid., 11
xliv Ibid.
xlv Ibid.
xlvi SportingNews, "Braves vs. Cardinals Wild Card Game delayed after controversial call," accessed July 1, 2013, http://www.sportingnews.com/mlb/story/2012-10-05/braves-cardinals-wild-card-game-delayed-after-controversial-call.
xlvii espnW, "Fans cheering after Cassel's injury inexcusable," accessed June 12, 2013, http://espn.go.com/espnw/news-commentary/article/8482084/espnw-fans-cheering-injury-kansas-city-chiefs-qb-matt-cassel-inexcusable.

xlviii SportingNews, "Georgia's Robinson says house egged after loss," accessed August 2, 2013, http://onlineathens.com/dogbytes/football/2012-10-07/georgias-robinson-says-house-egged-after-loss.

xlix The website of the *San Diego Union-Tribune,* "Giants fan beaten at Dodger Stadium returns home," accessed July 12, 2013, http://www.utsandiego.com/news/2013/jun/13/giants-fan-beaten-at-dodger-stadium-returns-home.

l CivilityinAmerica.org

li Jerry L. Van Marter, "Faith leaders call for higher standard of public discourse," Presbyterian News Service, accessed May 12, 2013, http://www.pcusa.org/news/2012/9/25/Faith-leaders-call-for-higher-standard.

lii The website for the Insight Meditation Society, "Joseph Goldstein: Biography," http://www.dharma.org/joseph-goldstein.

liii John O'Malley, *What Happened at Vatican II* (Harvard: Harvard University Press, 2008), 306.

liv Art Markman, "Money can buy happiness if you spent it right," the website for *Psychology Today,* accessed July 1, 2013, http://www.psychologytoday.com/blog/ulterior-motives/201005/money-can-buy-happiness-if-you-spent-it-right.

lv Art Markman, "Not All Happiness Is the Same," the website for *Psychology Today,* accessed July 1, 2013, http://www.psychologytoday.com/blog/ulterior-motives/201207/not-all-happiness-is-the-same.

lvi Ibid.

lvii Ryan T. Howell, "What Is Happiness? Five Characteristics of Happy People," the website for *Psychology Today,* accessed July 1, 2013, http://www.psychologytoday.com/blog/cant-buy-happiness/201301/what-is-happiness-five-characteristics-happy-people.

lviii   The website for Dr. Christina Hibbert, "Living a Life of Purpose and Meaning: The Key to True Happiness," accessed July 12, 2013, http://www.drchristinahibbert.com/living-a-life-of-purpose-and-meaning-the-key-to-true-happiness/#_ftn5.

lix   Forum Quoteland, Mark Twain, accessed September 20, 2013, http://www.goodreads.com/quotes/525269-life-is-short-break-the-rules-forgive-quickly-kiss-slowly4.

lx   Helpguide.org, "Laughter is the Best Medicine: The Health Benefits of Humor and Laughter," accessed September 24, 2013, http://www.helpguide.org/life/humor_laughter_health.htm.

lxi   Ibid.

lxii   Mother Teresa and Brian Kolodiejchuk, *Mother Teresa: Come Be My Light; The Private Writings of the Saint of Calcutta* (New York: Doubleday, 2007) 336-337.

lxiii   Ibid.

lxiv   Vikram Karve, "The Art of Smuggling," Sulekha.com (blog), accessed July 12, 2013, http://creative.sulekha.com/the-art-of-smuggling_79943_blog.

www.ingramcontent.com/pod-product-compliance
Lightning Source LLC
Chambersburg PA
CBHW020500030426
42337CB00011B/169